paint me a dream

by John Mc Guckin

John Mc Guckin

Original title
paint me a dream

Cover design
Sonja Smolec

Layout & graphics
Sonja Smolec, Yossi Faybish

Published by
Aquillrelle

Copyright 2011
All rights reserved - © John Mc Guckin

No part of this book may be reproduced or transmitted in any form or by any means, graphic, electronic, or mechanical, including photocopying, recording, taping, or by any information storage retrieval system, without the permission, in writing, from the publisher.

ISBN 978-1-4467-7441-0

Table of Contents

paint me a dream

No Regrets...15
One More Time...16
Belfast"...17
Empty Sky..18
Listening to Time...19
I Forgot..20
The Wind Has Stopped..21
Frost...22
Real-Time..23
Longing..24
Troubadour..25
It Matters...26
Street People..27
Mystery of the Heart..28
Frailty of Age...29
Silent Walking...30
Nearly Man..31
Man of Sighs..32
Timelines...33
Moving on in a Song..34
Saville Justice and Injustice.....................................35
Silent...38
You Know..39
Across the Line..40
It Was Good to See You...41
Silent Chair...42
Relax...43
Old Friend...44
Enola Gay..45
Selfishness...46
Shadows in Time...47
Change..48
Blame It on Your Phone..49

Old Times	50
Hallelujah	51
War	53
Un-Forgotten	54
Orange Fest, 11th Night	55
Angels	56
Searching	57
Believe in the Soul	58
Workers	59
Night Out	60
Loving Life	61
Why Not	62
Up the Road	63
G.D.E. Degree	64
The Last Bonfire	65
Belfast Giants	66
Snarling People	67
Land of Dreams	68
Bombay Street, Belfast 1969	69
Sunday Streets	71
Invisible Hoods	72
Rhythm of the Sky	73
Tender Love	74
Ireland's Warriors	75
Homewards	76
Do Nothing	78
Lifelines	79
One Wonders	81
Resources	82
On Angels' Wings	83
Adversity of Vanity	84
Die Sighing	86
Never Did	87
Hungover	88
Bag of Hammers	89
Talking Love	90
Fearful	91
Silence	92
When You Were a Young Girl	93
Losing You	94

Madness of Customers	95
Redemption Road	96
Playing in the Dust	97
Useless Mutterings	98
One World	99
Four Dollar Man	100
Here and Now	101
They Were Kids	102
Resentment	103
The Brow of the Hill	104
I Cannot Weep for America	105
Lilyana	106
The Man at the Door	107
Lights Out	108
Paint Me a Dream	109
Frozen Words	110
Random Man	111
Aussie Made	112
And Now - A Word from Brian	113
Grey Men	114
And All That There	115
Thanks to You	116
This Place	117
Hobby Horse	119
Computer Deaths	120
Happiness	121
Tomorrows	122
Telling	123
Rage	124
Legacy	125
Pair of Socks	126
Can't	127
Journeying	128
If	129
Dancing, with Lies	130
Dreams Are Not Enough	131
Drinking	132
Perspective	133
Yesterday	134
Being Me	135
Strolling	136

Dance of Firs	137
Living and Hoping	138
Last Night	139
Tin Hat Days	140
Belfast, Two	141
Easy Thinking	142
Believe in the Soul, Two	143
Avarice	144
Cast a Long Shadow	145
Never Alone	146
Was Thinking	147
Knaves Laughing	148
Empty Arms	149
Reflections of a Woman	150
Peaceful Lady	151
Nothing	152
Lost in a Familiar Place	153
A life Well Lived	154
Heroin Nights	155
Echo Man	156
Autumn Drumlins	157
Abandoned	158
Back Again	159
Paedophile Man	160
Assumption	161
Garage Rules	162
Simply You	163
Simplicity	164
Drifting	165
Evensong	166
Spirit	167
Emma's Day Out	168
Old Times / New Times	169
Broken Leaves	170
Broken Strings	171
Players	172
Hoods Morality	173
Face Value	174
Today's Wigan Pier / A Parody of Orwell	175
Halloween	176

Because of You	177
Mr. and Mrs. Blah	178
Moonlight	179
Longing	180
Letter in a Box	181
Dancing in the Shadow of the Wind	182
Mumbia	183
Belfast, City of Madness	184
Fateful Night	185
Back When	186
Angels Caring	188
I Wonder	189
Echoes	190
American Diplomacy	191
Waltz	192
Indifferent	193
Weary	194
Serious	195
Today is Different	196
Unseen	197
Wasted Lives	198
Big City Time	199
Flight	200
Life, Maybe, Perhaps	201
Why	202
Don't Think	203
Yesterday's Man	204
Immigrants' Souls	205
The Burning Man	207
Hi	209
Immoralist	210
Nuclear	211
Love Never Ages	212
Dark Night	213
Awhile	214
Hidden Valley / Alice Springs, 2006	215
Once in Belfast	216
Relentless	217
Smile	218
To Have Lived the Dream	219
Moments in Time	220

A Terrible Beauty 221
Imprint My Love 222
Shake Hands with My Heart 223
No Man's Land 224
Truth 225
No Epitaph 226
Provisional Honour 227
Love Redeems All 228
One More Night 229

dedications:

— to my beautiful daughters - Karen, Joanne and Emma, to my wonderful grandchildren - all seven of them, and to my former wife - Geraldine, the one who put up with me for 25 years.

— to my dear friends Joe Rafferty, the humble man, and Maggie Kerr from far-away Australia, the lady with a beautiful mind.

— to Mr. Noel Maguire, for his fair and honest critique.

— a special dedication to wee Liz, the wonderful lady who taught me about life and love, sadly passed away 25th July, 2004. Sweet wee Liz - your spirit lives on in all who loved you.

paint me a dream

No Regrets

Watching and admiring the shifting
Sands of time, allows me to reflect
On all those times I thought were adversity
Now looking askance at the shifting sands of time
I realise those moments were only the making
Of the man, I cannot, nor will ever refute
The wonders of days spent living and
Loving, the moments that only make up a life,
Now I stand at the tide of time with
No regrets or recriminations, simply an acceptance of
God's hand in helping me shift the never ending sands of time

One More Time

Say goodbye to love.
One more time I try to recall all the
Silly things said, and unsaid, why say
I love you then say I don't love you
Striking out in hurt or embarrassment?

Why not state one more time
Girl - I love you, leave it alone,
Enjoy the time together, why say goodbye
When each time you want to stay,
Hold her and say sorry, not too hard
Even if you are full of self, thinking I'm right.
Even when you are right, you are wrong.

One time when you reach out
She shall have fled forever all because
You thought you were more important.
When you go to sleep alone imagine
Having one more time to make it right
Holding her tight, and saying - girl, I love you.

Belfast

Belfast, once a mighty industrial city
Dormant now, you wait the new dawning
One that knows you would never deny,
Your people toiled from dawn to dusk accomplishing the
Strength that makes a city grow in mind and spirit,
The hearts and soul of your people standing steadfast with you.

Belfast, at times cast as a terrible beauty
Though in its streets walk proud people,
People such as half timers who wrought in the mills,
Shipyard men and aircraft builders, a divided city
Cut in two by the Lagan flow, one side Down the other Antrim,
Then Divis Mountain with its rivers that fed the growth of mills,
Now all lie corrosive, the industry of Belfast disappeared.

Belfast, the landfall of its lough launched many ships
Famous and infamous, this grim city holds all in hock
Though they have redeemed themselves many times,
Lying smug in its verdant valley it plays host to myriad guests
Who visit and exclaim in wonderment upon Castlereagh hills
And Black Mountain whilst we, the people, distain
Our pride of Belfast Town, this now living City.

Empty Sky

Overhead, an empty sky.
Troubling me, seeking as I am
solace, a night's sky, devoid
of starlight, a reflective moon in
teardrop shape that has waned into
crying shame. Its benign glance
shimmering across oceans, smiling
upon golden harvests, alas can not be seen.
And I, weary, stretching to touch the
sky, feel only its bluesteel core.
Coldness grips me, as I yearn
for beauty's comforting touch.
Would, if I could, embrace the sky,
become lost in its beguiling
moods. Find solace in moonlight's whey.
Tread once again amongst starlight
and accept infinity's depths as my
will-o-the-wisp, weep no more
for beauty, lost in an empty sky...

Listening to Time

Time can be likened to a teardrop
On the cheek of the world, let's reflect
On old and new moments of time in
Our everyday lives that benefit or enhance
The meek in this beautiful world.

Moments in time we sometimes take no notice of
And miss the beauty of life, a newborn child's cry
The sound of love is heard if we listen, learn to accept
Any adversity that befalls the child who,
In time, comes to live in our hearts, listening to
That child lets us hear the sound of love.
In its cries lies the beauty of life

Welcome winter and summer into your time,
All love filled memories children remember,
Give thanks for everyday they spend with you
Lend your moments in time gracefully, and
You shall find peace reigning within your mind.

Time is fleeting, and as the teardrop can be
Wiped away so too can happiness.
We all need to live in the day seeking to
Make good use of our lives reaching out
To those we love, and say I love you.

I Forgot

What did I forget? How to laugh,
Most importantly I forgot
how to say no.
No to most of the useless demands
That being married
Heaps upon you,
in the midst of doing things.

You lose sight of yourself.
All you have is a worried mind,
laughter an alien sound you hear,
and think I used to do that.
What happened? Forgot to laugh.
Just took life too seriously
And started to live a lie.

Not the lie of family.
They are all important. Simply
Thinking okay, you want more,
I'll go out and get more.

In today's society we want,
what do we want?
More, that we don't need,
And we forget to laugh.

Dickens stated it years ago.
Earn sixpence save
A penny, happiness.
Spend nine pence, unhappiness.

The Wind Has Stopped

The wind has stopped blowing, there is
A sense of stillness in people's minds.
Time to think upon life and all its hardships.
When we let ourselves be blown here and there
By any whim that takes us, we forget
Life, and do as we like, we treat life as a waltz,
With all the grief that we have successfully
Cast into the wind: death, sickness, disability.

Our friends were caught up in their cold winds of life
As we blithely went our own merry way riding
That carousel to nowhere. Time now that the
Wind has stopped blowing to look around, reach out,
Our arms give life a hug, and help a friend.
Offer to listen, and hold their problems in our hearts.
Offer solace, let them know how much we love them.

The winds shall once again blow, and then
It could be a cold, cold wind with not a friend in your life.
If you let the wind blow you here and there
It becomes so difficult to utter these simple words,
Hello again, I love you, and missed you.

Frost

Web etched in whiteness.
Dead briars awaiting
Spring's renewal,
Cold, minus cold, gripping
The land, fog, endless fog.

In its smokey coldness
Unseen voices glide past.
All that is heard are thick soled boots
Pushing through its silken void
Carrying echoes of spring's renewal.
When once again, we watch dead briars
Once more embrace the springtime

Now only lifeless housing estates.
Their windows shrouded in fog.
Listening for crunching boots,
Spider thoughts of no wages, winter
Limned in frost, spring seems so far away.

Depressing winter - fog, frost,
Absent of sunlight to burn it all away.
Only the sounds of working boots
Straying despairingly homewards.
No work, only minus cold and freezing fog.

Real-Time

This is just another night.
Glue cans are in use
In real-time.
Stars and clouds drifting about.
Year's end, no answer to real-time.
Only drink and drugs make sense.

TV on mute, street music on loud.
Simply another night, at year's end.
Let's hang out, and drift about.
No questions asked, no answers to give.
This is real-time in, every City.

Longing

I glanced away
And you were gone, Liz.
As if an early mist
Had been burned away
By morning sunlight.

Though knowing within my soul
You had roiled away
Into God's all forgiving embrace.
I wandered and watched
Until night drew in.
Then I chanced upon the stars.

You, my darling girl,
Had reappeared,
Laughing mischievously
Among the starlight,
I glance away
And when I glance back

You are still there,
On diamond nights
You can always be seen,
Dancing, laughing, and
Playing, amongst the starlight.

Troubadour

The troubadour remains, motionless.
A single tear staining his makeup,
The curtain slowly closing destroys
His reason for living: the audience.
Suddenly the magic's gone,

Leaving only despair: reality.
The warped boards that only
Moments ago, were his to command.
Each night this moment arrives.
Countless days spent, dreading the ending.
Endless days, stretching into
The final act: obscurity.

Glamour, mayhem, spent on stage.
The troubadour, alone, is motionless.
Movement pointless, no audience to applaud and
Caress his ego, each performance
Means movement, the dreaded end: despair.

As the troubadour stares once more stares
Into the abyss of loneliness, not for him
Life's true meaning of love,
Joy, and companionship.
The troubadour, alone,
Always finds life joys beyond reach.

It Matters

It doesn't matter what time
You were born, or when you
Wandered off to find a life.

It only matters that, along the way
You did what was right.
All your partner and family needed
You caused it to happen, through hard work.

In your time you were needed.
Now, weary, time supplants energy.
Loneliness, age's wicked weapon.
Staring at a TV screen.

Then think, maybe I should walk.
Talk to people I meet. After all
The slight time I have left might matter,
No gain in giving up, after all.
A hello costs no effort, maybe cheers me up
Hearing myself say hello again, hello.

Street People

Have you ever walked past street people,
Averted your eyes, and wondered
Why don't they work? Can't.
Life's injustices heaped upon them,
They cannot cope.

Their deep vacant eyes staring, see nothing.
Maybe if we stopped and said hello, that kind word
Could, momentarily, change their world.
To much hurt, and they gave up.

Next time you pass by, stop and drop a coin
In their cup, though maybe a kind word
Is worth a thousand coins, who knows?
Gaze upon them as people, not drop outs.

Simply people who could not cope,
with society's indifferent attitudes.
Gaze quietly upon those vacant eyes
And remember -

They are a people.

Mystery of the Heart

Free the heart of painful parting.
Let old loves Enter our mind and
Set free the roll of honour of
All our friends who have died.

Remembering them whether in pain or joy.
It is this the mystery of the heart.
It will never be defeated, even when
We acknowledge our loved ones are gone.
This all embracing mystery
Is simple to accept, all you have to do
Or to have done, is to love.

In The mystery of the heart
The beauty is that it can
Always return to loving life's friendships,
And in that simple fact we can
Accept that the heart shall always
Remain attuned to being... a mystery.

Frailty of Age

The bloom of youth has long been swept away,
Today we just accept the truth.
That I, we, cannot do that
Which we expect of ourselves.

Sad though true is the frailty of age, it need not
Be too old an age, sometimes the limits
Of our endurance were pushed beyond
Normal expectations, and today we have to accept,
We can no longer be the men/women we once were.

If in this time, when our flesh
Is looser, and flabbier
WE retain a modicum of good health, then,
All we need say is *Thank You God*.
For all the good times you gave us.

Silent Walking

Silent walking stretches memory
Into sunnier youthful times.
Playing hide and seek, stealing stealthily along,
Shouting boo, you're on it.

Playing once again games of innocence.
Cherished sounds of laughter found in
Childish glee chasing wraiths of self.
Fleeting forms scampering happily away,
And I, cheerfully enjoying the silent walking,

As it jolts consciousness back experiencing
Other innocent games played, in mesmerizing
Golden times that fade, with each new dawn.
Silent walking with grandchildren, realising
I'm not too old to play.

Childish shouts, inspiring youth albeit, momentary,
Receding glances of sepia boyhood
Brought forwards into middle age chasing children,
And you, realising these are their silent walking moments
Knowing one day they *will* glance back
Into childhood years.

Nearly Man

I met a man the other day.
He called himself the nearly man.
I asked him, why do you call yourself
The nearly man? He answered
I was nearly good at sport,
I was nearly good at loving,
Nearly good at being a husband,
Heck, I was nearly good at living.
Though, just fell short at being good
At anything. So I became the nearly man.
The nearly man, afraid of failure,
Dreams his dreams, those actions
Never quite achieved, living out his time
In books wishing he was the always man.
Now he has resigned himself to
His role in life, to always being
The nearly man.

Man of Sighs

Gazing sorrowfully upon man's folly
The man of sighs dies, knowing
Man's cruelty to man shall never cease
It will leave him despairing
Throughout the eons of time.

If 9/11 was our day of tears his was Golgotha,
Crucified by man, held erect by nails, he forgave
The mourning crowd, even the centurion who
Drove the spear into his side, though we did at that moment
Create this world of sighs,
Places such as Flanders fields,
Auschwitz, Vietnam, Palestine, Rwanda,

The man of sighs lived through each enormity
In his forgiveness great is his pity, knowing
That his creation commits such dastardly acts
Again, and again creating this,
Our singular world of sighs.

Timelines

We are all born with an allotted time.
Therefore live life to its fullest.
We have only this time, it remains constant
Use it wisely do not put off telling those
You love, that you do love them, remember,

Appreciation should be expressed as well as felt.
Spend your time and everyone's time kindly,
Live in the now, though learn to plan ahead
Hopefully you shall have tomorrow's time,
Use it wisely.

Do not waste time judging others you have never
Walked in their shoes, help one another to extend
Love in all our time. Love is, and should be constant
In all your time, in God's grace use it wisely

Treat love with respect and loyalty.
Remember, we only have this one timeline.
Grow old gracefully, knowing you have
Lived your time here on earth wisely.

Moving on in a Song

Play me a song, don't think
About the title.
Just play me a song.

One from your heart, let me think
I still mean something to you.
Even if it tears me apart.
Go on, play me a song.

Let me imagine sweeping plains,
Lingering evening sunsets, living my dreams,
Go on, play me a song.
Any song, just one that doesn't hurt.
Let me think you still love me.

In the words of a song I know
You're moving on, go, move right along,
Pack your bag say so long.
It was good to know you even if
All I ended up with are the words of a song.

Saville Justice and Injustice

38 years, a moment in time.
A white kerchief held aloft by a cleric called Edward Daly.
Not a flag of surrender, only a signal
That a wounded man was receiving last rites.

13 dead, murdered on the day whilst another
Lingered in hospital, the inevitable happened, he died
14 killed, by British paratroopers.
Many score lay wounded, as the forces of the crown
Kept murdering and shooting innocent people,
Even as they lay on the ground.
An echo of despair, reverberated around the world.

Horror, shock, that this is happening on a
British street is unthinkable.

Until lord chief justice Widgery was told
In no uncertain terms, brand them all
Gunmen and bombers, the creditability of those
Innocent dead in Derry besmirched by another British lackey.

The truth was told at a press conference 2 hours after the outrage,
They were only children
Fleeing the rampage of murdering thugs sent in to sort out the problem.

That dastardly problem lay
In the peaceful protest of asking for civil rights.
It was accepted as right and proper by the world press
But, the British prideful government decried no,
"We are an honourable people".

It did not happen, they were all guilty of a crime carrying arms
And so the injustice of British justice witnessed
In full view of British TV cameras,

Guns, bombs none were ever recovered
From the victims, they did not exist.
Now 38 moments past, each day a year
For every grieved family until 15 of June 2010
They were cleared of being terrorists

Now Edward Daly, and the world press ask
Where are the official photographs taken at Rossville flats
38 long years before showing they were the innocents
Sacrificed by British might? Destroyed to sustain the
So called honour of British right to spend.
200 million pounds to sustain a lie depicted here
In the list of the dead and injured.

List of those killed:

Patrick ('Paddy') Doherty (31)
Gerald Donaghy (17)
John ('Jackie') Duddy (17)
Hugh Gilmour (17)
Michael Kelly (17)
Michael McDaid (20)
Kevin McElhinney (17)
Bernard ('Barney') McGuigan (41)
Gerald McKinney (35)
William ('Willie') McKinney (26)
William Nash (19)
James ('Jim') Wray (22)
John Young (17)
John Johnston (59)
(John Johnson was shot twice on 30 January 1972 and died on 16 June 1972. His family is convinced that he died prematurely and that his death was due to the injuries received and trauma he underwent on 'Bloody Sunday'.)

List of those injured (from gunfire, unless otherwise stated):

Michael Bradley (22)
Michael Bridge (25)
Alana Burke (18)
(injured when run down by a British Army armoured personnel carrier)
Patrick Campbell (53)

(injured when run down by a British Army armoured personnel carrier)
Margaret ('Peggy') Derry (37)
(the only woman shot and injured on 'Bloody Sunday')
Damien Donaghy (15)
Joseph ('Joe') Friel (20)
Daniel Gillespie (31)
(not mentioned in Widgery's Tribunal Report)
Joseph Mahon (16)
Patrick McDaid (24)
Daniel McGowan (37)
Alexander ('Alex') Nash (52)
Patrick ('Paddy') O'Donnell (41)
Michael Quinn (17)

Silent

Words of silence
Seek peace within
The depths of my solitude
Resonating through my mind
Images swimming in timelessness
Have me holding you

Yet once again knowing
You only exist in my mind
Though I shall hold your memories close
Whilst listening to words of silence.

Dancing into my dreams wraith like
You appear, and I can hold only shadows
Of you in my mind whilst listening
To words of silence.

You Know

You know, I met yer man
The other day, you know
Yer man, of course you do.

Everybody knows him, you know.
Who, what's his name it's, you know
Anyway I asked him about you, you know.
He said he didn't know you, now I find that
A bit strange coming from, you know
Anyway we talked about you, you know.
Who, yer man lives down the road, you know.

On his own, he lives, you know, yer man
You mean to tell me you don't know, you know
O well I'll just go, and talk to
Yer other man you know him!!
He always knows. You know.

Annoying Belfast colloquial phrase, you know.

Across the Line

Many lines are finely drawn,
In Belfast town it is hard to know when you have crossed from one divide
Into another dimension of hate and bigotry.

A name, a place, an incident spoken in the wrong place at the wrong time
Earns you the eternal right to be killed in the unspoken law of bigotry
Simply because you strayed across the line into our area.
Do you belong in it?
A Jewish catholic, Hindu catholic, protestant Jew
Or Hindu protestant it does not matter.

You are not one of us. Who are we?
We are the people, and we hate everyone
No discrimination, we just hate all of you
We have huffed, and we puffed
Blew your lives away, tortured, and slaughtered
Especially in the romper room on a pleasant Sunday morning, having a wee drink before church.

Belfast, Belfast we love our town
You are very welcome
As long as you do not stray across the line
Once you do, you will be lucky
Lucky, if we the people let you leave walking
Remember, this is our town
Do not stray across the line.

* *This is Belfast 2010, not 1920. Nothing changes. In a whirlpool of changes, Procul Harem got it right in the 1960 era.*
* *Romper room refers to a drinking club where innocent people where taken and tortured, then murdered in the name of God and country. Makes one pause and think.*

It Was Good To See You

Why did you have to go?
Guess, I'll never know.
Simply have to say, cheerio,
And let you go though, please,
I don't want you going away.

Can't you stay, even if it's
Only for a wee while, please,
Please, I beg you to stay, only
For one more day, I know you
Don't want to go, why God called
You, guess I'll never know.

Thankfully, you left me with this thought,
And it helps each, and every day.
In that hospital bed, when you said
It was so good to see you.
Wherever you are, in that silent land
I know you loved me, why
Did you have to go, guess I'll never know.

You where the embodiment of goodness, wee Liz.

Silent Chair

Silent chair, in this silent room,
States all the facts that remain
Deeply felt.
Lonely nights, lonely days.
Unspoken thoughts.

Hidden from my silent self.
What are the facts, lets see.
No one to listen to or hear my
Unspoken dreams, clearly felt
Then left to grace, an empty shelf.

Prowling around that silent room
I scream and shout, who's to hear?
Only a silent chair listening to my
Unspoken dreams of yesteryear.

Relax

Relax, calm down, come to your senses.
Remember your year happens in one day.
Let life become your passion, don't fight it.
Go with the flow and let yourself drift on
Clouds of gold, your life changes in one day.

You may try to change it, better to let reality
Be your mentor, and relax, your day happens,
Go with it, run with the wind, lie in the sun,
You may encounter destroyed spirits,
Their problems are not yours, seize the day.
Keep free and relax, no matter what happens,
It's only one day.

Keep peace in your soul, love in your heart,
And joy shall enter your spirit, relax.
Remember your year happens in one day.
All you can do is go with the flow
And enjoy being alive.

Old Friend

Good bye old friend, Good bye.
The years flew past so quickly
Old Friend.
Though only five really counted,
That's when I held you
Old Friend.
We didn't get to say goodbye.
I really should have been there
To hold you. Thirty seven years
We should have held one another.
Could have relied upon each other
Old Friend.
Goodbye my friend, goodbye.
In dreams, at least, I hold you
And say hello again, hello.
My dear, my darling dear
Old Friend. Wee Liz.

Enola Gay

Was Manhattan worth
The shadow on the wall?
This travesty of power
Destroyed twin cities
Of dreams.

A bomb valued
More than millions of lives?
Eternity shall - with good reason
Condemn America's selfishness
Creating generations of shadows.

Torn buildings remain,
Mute monuments to a selfish act
Destroying their credibility.
Though, building better bombs
Underscores the Manhattan
Project's aim

I imagine perpetuity shall
Remember those endearing names
Little boy, big boy, denoting
The worst act of terrorism
Our world has ever known.

Selfishness

Standing, staring at vast
Fields of flowers, you let your
Gaze focus on one solitary stem.
As if, in those vast fields, only one
Petal exists, and its reality is there
Only for you.

Forgetting life is all around, engulfing everyone.
You focus, on that one stem one solitary petal,
It allows you to let reality blow away, as the
Wind ripples across, these vast fields.
Thinking nothing of all the lives locked away, in
Happiness or penury, let them into your heart,
Look upon the world with wonder.

Hear each soft sigh, as the wind bends those
Delicate stalks - each lament, every shout of happiness.
Let each stem, each petal, become as one with you.
There, in your mind, decide to help others through
Adversity, and in doing so, those vast fields
Of flowers shall engulf your soul
And you will find peace of mind.

Shadows in Time

Dancing with shadows.
Waltzing with memories.
Slow steps in time
Seeing shadows in my mind.

Dance into the light.
Step into the shade.
Slow steps in time
Remind me of sweet memories

Held in my mind and
Now, as I dance with time,
Holding life in my palms
Stepping into the shade
Waltzing into the light.

I let life's music carry me back
To golden memories when I danced
A dream which seemed never ending.

Now shuffling to
Slow steps in time
All I hold are those memories
As I waltz with my dreams to
Slow steps in time.

Change

Change is akin to pushing water uphill.
Wanting things to remain the same, but
Always events flow around, bewildering at times
Then, everything slows to normal and why,
Because we plugged the dam of our emotions.

Not adverse to change, accepting
Why I decided it was time for change,
Needing to pay attention
To the tenet that change
Only comes from within, and as long
As I remain true to my emotions.

Change, and the unnecessary feeling
Of pushing water uphill
Can be dealt with, instead of struggling
Let's float as if
In clear pools where
The water has stilled.

Blame It on Your Phone

Stumbling, mumbling prayers of self pity.
Peering at a tracking device, searching for solace
In a forgotten number, pressing buttons uncaringly.
Sharing no thought for others, only self pitied righteousness.

Swearing into dead space I'm right, of course I'm right.
Studying wreckage of past life remembered
In a forgotten number, scolding at a tracking device,
Message found lost, in drafts, plastic technology,
Drop it into big uncaring City Sewer, can only wonder
Where it's going, don't care, won't have to share.

Stumble onwards into dead space, blaming the phone.
Thinking of a message once sent, damning you,
Declaring in your mind the phone is the fault.
No blame, no shame, when you can
Cover your tracks, simply by dropping the device.
Wander onwards into a nowhere life.

Old Times

Evening prose
Quietly spoken
Between chairs
And tables,
Talk quietly
Of evenings.
When people
Strolled, arm in arm.
A time of life
Now gone
Into history.

Hallelujah

Hallelujah, Hallelujah,
Here we are, celebrating
Our Christian culture once again,
It's the twelfth day
Let's march, sorry,
Trample triumphantly over
The Catholic communities,
Hold our banners of old ideologies aloft.

It all may have happened
In 1690, when? 1690.
That's so long ago,
No it's not, in our minds of hate.
It happened today.
That's why we march letting "them"
Know we always will declare,

No surrender that means
There shall not be peace
In our time, you know
It's true that everything we do
Is for God, and country,
Our God, not your God.
The one old red socks, and you revere.

Hallelujah, hallelujah,
It's our day of hate, once again
Let's get drunk, light bonfires
And celebrate our culture,
Generally destroy our own
Communities with blazing rubbish.
After all, we are the "people".

Degenerate force backed up by
A protestant parliament.
Beat those lambeg drums
Until our wrists bleed and
Then listen at the field to
Rhetoric of hate, Hallelujah, Hallelujah.
Our day of culture dawns,
It's the twelfth once again...

War

Who is right, who is wrong?
In God's mind we all are at fault.
To say God bless our soldiers seems
A travesty of God's love for all of his creations.
Who is right, the one who states he is.

The one who commits the worst atrocities,
The governments who declare we will fight,
The terrorist who declares I'm right, and we shall fight.
None of them in God's mind is right,
Thou shall not kill seems to be a forgotten commandment of all,
Our one God. Why do we not demand of governments
To look to our past to see clearly our future?

Shall we forever waste the lives of our young men
And women? Give us peace, this word appears
To breed abhorrence in all our leaders.
Peace in our time, when is it to be?
Never it seems, we waste all
These lives, and our egoistical leaders
Bow their heads as the strains of the last post.
Ring out, ask them
Do you cry for these young people?
If you do then stop killing, and maiming,
In God's name - *stop!*

Un-Forgotten

Years have drifted by, and the
Weeds have grown high above your
Grave, and you, having passed through
Heavens gate, know you have not laid forgotten,
Your soul carried on, yet I, could not settle.

Roamed around seeking to meet with you once again,
Could not accept God's decision to embrace you.
Now that peace has entered my soul, I can stand
Were your shadows lie all around, and let memories
Of your wisdom flood into the river of my mind.
I have spoken with you in dreams, though always
I would not accept, and believe in the soul.

Now as I sweep these weeds aside, I realise the only
One who was never with you was me. Upon accepting
That you are with our God, peace, contentment, and
Happiness had entered my soul ceasing my roaming.
The weeds shall never grow steadily ever again, knowing
And accepting that all is as it should be, you are living
The life we are all promised: eternity.

Orange Fest, 11th Night

Orange fest in Belfast Town, glorious
Firelight to stain the night's sky, as once
Again we burn their Irish green, white and gold flag,
That effigy of the pope, cheer as we watch it burn
Wishing with all the hate in our hearts it was him.

Bonfire night declaring we are British.
Such a nonsense term even the English,
Scottish, and Welsh who live on the island
Of England do not say we are British, only
These moronic hate filled loyalists cry, no surrender,
We are British is their war cry, reality is that they
Are Irish, politically manipulated people.

No industry to sustain them, all lost to
The tide of time, now they walk the dole line
Weeping into their bonfire, but we are the people
Are we not? No, nor ever were, just fodder for politicians
Who quietly lined their own pockets with
Irish and English money, cheer, get drunk, and
Watch your heritage turn to ashes. It's great to be British.

Angels

Even angels can't smile always,
Often times they relax and let you smile for them.

It's their way of carrying you
Through a sad, or bad day.

Let's have a smile and light up an angel's day,
It's a special moment when that smile lets your angel sigh and walk with you.

An angel shall always be by your side.

Searching

If all things come to pass
Maybe one day we shall be
Able to learn about trust and love,
On the journey of living
We can find ourselves by helping others.

In doing so trust love, it brings peace.
We will find our elusive grail urging us
Onwards to the land of hope and glory,
Others you meet on the same roadway
Will reach out to you, embrace them, wrap
All of them in your spirit, and the Holy Grail
Of God's simple gift becomes clear: love.

Hand it over to love and accept God's
Wisdom no harm will befall you, we are
All on the one journey towards eternity,
The roadway ahead has become clear -
Humility, peace, love, found in acceptance.

Believe in the Soul

Wherever I may roam you shall
Always remain safely held
In my heart, today and forever,
Onwards we are as one, believe in
The soul, it is forever steadfast.

The soul marches to a different beat.
We can neither see nor hear it but
Always, if we believe in the soul, its
Presence is forever felt and you can
Find peace in your mind knowing
That one day we shall all be together.

The spirit of your loved one is as
Unwavering as the North Star,
Always there to guide you through
The trials and tribulations of life.
Believe in the soul.

Workers

The jib swings to and fro,
Its cold metal indifferent to
Its minions below, from its vantage
Point it watches, and notes the
Daily hurts and vices of the workers below.
Slinging, heaving, they feed the jib
Each day. This daily ritual as the
Worker struggles from 8am to 6pm
Whilst above them, and the jib,
Stand the bosses.

Night Out

Phone for a taxi, step
Lightly to the door
And tap gently upon it,
When answered step inside,
Gaze in wonderment and awe
That this beautiful woman
Is going out with you.
Escort her to the taxi
Settle her gently inside
Then float dreamlike beside her
You and she are going out together.

Loving Life

Spending every moment of every
Hour on the road loving life, that's what I do.
That's all, I am a lover of life.
Drifting along down highways and byways
Maybe some day I will get it right and
Stop of somewhere, don't know where.

Doesn't matter so long as I keep on
Keeping on, loving life what can go wrong?
Keep a smile on your face, a few good friends close
And of course any enemy's closer still.
Loving life is a God given gift. I won't want to waste it
Cursing and judging others over some imagined slight.
No time to do anything but smile and help other drifters along.

Our thoughts may not be beguiling but, walking along,
Sharing a smile, our last smoke or even a drink
Doing so I shall forever be in love with life.
Don't want no office job, no wife.
I'm keeping it simple, smiling and drifting along
Enjoying this life in my own easy, crazy way.

Why Not

Why not, why not what, I don't know,
Just accept what I got may not be a lot
But there is no good keeping on asking.
Why me, I ask, why not me, you, could be
Anyone.

Out there are a lot of people, many colours,
Many tongues, lot of them doing good, a lot
Not so good, and we ask ourselves why not.
On the one hand dictatorship, legacy of the white man
Forgot he is part of the human race, only race there is.
Because of power and the colour of his white skin
He thinks why not, he's better than you, me, and us.

Ask yourself why not us, lot of wonders in God's world,
We got a right to take a bite, why not,
Get off our knees let us rise, the great are only great
Because we are on our knees, lot of fancy sayings
They work if we listen and make them work for us.
And why not every day we do nothing is a dismal day
For all of us, and why not if we won't reach out
This great world is for all, and why not?

Up the Road

Remember days playing games
Into long bright nights, old familiar
Games played happily shouting
Rallyo, rallyo who's got the ball,
And wee Doll's playing three balls
Against an adjacent wall.

Innocent times, Queenio, queenio who's got
The ball. We should have tried to keep those
Times in our pockets. I believe we lost our marleys
When living streets where razed, gone down the
Road of rubble. We left the characters behind
Singing for a few bob, working the picture queues
St Tawesa of de Woses the children called him beer bottle.

His name was John Donnelly, an inoffensive man.
We left it all behind as we moved up the road.
New homes, no more open doors
Only locked in, closed down living.

New estates, foreign living.
The living streets gone,
Recalled over a pint of
Stout when we sit reminiscing about
Those long, bright nights.

G.D.E. Degree

Used to be a joke went around, he's got
A G.D.E. degree, isn't he the responsible guy?
Now if you put your B.I.N. out on the street
With, god forbid, wrong garbage infill
That big man with his garbage disposal expert degree
Shall remonstrate most strongly with you as
He flicks through your garbage.

And, wonder of wonders, the years that we must appreciate
Perfecting that most perfect part of his G.D.E. is when he
Demonstrates his first class honours degree, pitch perfect
Tsk' Tsk'. Tsk'.

That's a first grade honours degree (reclamation)
On how you should display your garbage, after all
This man with his G.D.E. degree is your bin man,
Council paid him through the G.D.E. sites, and now
He is qualified to tell you how to fill your bin.
It's truly a wonderment to have a degree in G.D.E.

The Last Bonfire

The wood has been collected, stacked
And guarded, midnight of the eight day
Approaches, is this truly the last bonfire?
When flames roar skywards and people
Scream out about their pain of internment.

Can we truly believe it's the last bonfire?
On Marian day we lit them for years.
When voices were raised they did so in praise.
Perhaps if the eight night bonfire is truly the last
Then maybe somehow some day the painful
Memories of restless times will pass.

Let others light their bonfires, celebrate
Ancient moments in history, we cannot
Let antiquated hate become our future
Today, as the eighth day of midnight approaches.
Believe, in the last bonfire.

Belfast Giants

Living in this city, metal giants
Dominate our skyline. Creeping along
On ribbons of steel, building only ghost
Ships now. Giants named Samson and Goliath,
Waiting on Belfast to build real ships again.

Belfast once stood on giant shoulders forged
From its workers - women of the mills, men
Of the shipyards, factories supplying steel, linen,
Hemp, ships, aircraft, Belfast once walked tall.
Alongside mighty rumbling giants only
Samson and Goliath remain.

Now their ribbons of steel lie rusting, Belfast
Beckons, look at our history, mayhem of workers,
Pride helped cause our downfall, tears of rust stream
Down these mighty metal giants' flanks, time has passed
Them and Belfast by on progress' road.

Snarling People

Out the way, for Gods sake
Get out of my way, I'm in a hurry,
Nothing else matters only my wants,
Get out of my way, now! Living in the
City people snarl, under pressure can't stop.

No time for pity, city living a myth,
Its people abhor mercy, push, shove for
God's sake move, we want. Only problem
Living in the City we lose sight of our needs,
Love and compassion is forgotten.
Nothing speaks as eloquently as violence.
That's life, in the big city.

Land of Dreams

In this land of dreams where we dwell
In sleep, safe from harm, here everyone
Relives past times, and a future only they can see.
In our magical land of dreams all is peaceful.
No one is lonely, all anguish and hurt is cast aside.

In our land of dreams we stand together, at peace.
Let's carry our memories of those loved one as
Magical times to be brought alive from where we
Store them in our hearts. It's our land of dreams,
All and everything you need or want will be granted,
Especially the knowledge that you are protected
By God's love, in our wonderful land of dreams.

Bombay Street, Belfast, 1969

Human kindness dissipates in the flames of hate
As loyalist thugs ran the line to fire Bombay Street
Screaming out their primeval war cry
No Surrender!
The devil ran free that fateful day in '69
As he demonized
Worker against worker,
same future,
same past.

Working men listening to politicians' rhetoric,
Fat cats regurgitating lies against
(Catholics) Nationalists,
Only want an all Ireland shore,
Sun went down on that old sore in 1922,
Protestant, Catholic, all of them workers
"United"
Wouldn't do to let the worker know
They can have dignity.

Burning homes lets us know
We are winning the fight
Against workers' plight Catholic's voting
one man
one vote
never.
Run the line of Bombay St, burn, burn the homes.
Put those Shorland armoured cars on city streets,
open fire, light up the night sky with tracer rounds, and
we don't cry as Patrick Rooney is shot
dead in bed

(nine years of age, first child to die)

Does not matter, we are winning the fight.
That demonized war cry, No Surrender, from politicians.
Loyalist triumphalism,
this is our land,
Six counties of Ulster.
We walk the line in the blood of innocents as 1505 families
Flee their homes. And so the 40 years of the troubles began.

Six counties of Ulster shall never lie in the arms of the angels.

Sunday Streets

There's a time for you, even when
You feel you are all alone expecting
Nothing from anyone, walking on deserted
Sunday streets as twilight arrives, it seems as if
There is no hope for you but love waits for you,
It can arrive, as you walk alone on deserted Sunday streets.

Every step you take someone is walking the same path.
Maybe beyond the horizon your future is strolling
Same as you, and your time in life is about to happen,
In the soft evening twilight your reason for being there
Is about to unfold, it lies just beyond your horizon
When you turn that corner and your time arrives to fall in
Love, you realise that deserted Sunday is destiny.

Invisible Hoods

Invisible men, living in invisible minds
Creating very visible crimes, living
Incredibly insipid lives, existence,
Preening in front of invisible peers, though
We all realise you are nothing men.

Such lonely times when you're an invisible hood.
Walk along your invisible path, strut and preen,
Pity you don't realize you're
An invisible man, out on your own, perhaps
One day you'll cast aside your visible crimes
And walk alongside very visible men.
You're the nowhere man, totally invisible.

Rhythm of the Sky

Gossamer valleys,
Mountainous peaks,
Looking upwards
Only the plane and
The freedom of the sky.
Above the clouds, I stare
Towards infinity.
Horizons flow past, cast
In golden brown hues.
Flying from sunset to sunrise
Rhythms of the sky beguile.
Only God is above,
And the green golden Earth
Lies far below.
Vast landscapes slip into
Blue green oceans, seemly
Cradling mother Earth,
And I sit and watch a
Never-ending portrait
Of God's beauty
As I travel onwards-
Towards my home.

Tender Love

You are in love, and trying to
Make it work whilst, unknown to you,
He plays at charades. Sonnets of love

Talked about, though in his mind, you
Where already cast aside.
Flotsam, drifting on the tide of love.
Your precious time wasted.

All the while you tried, didn't tire.
But, knowing deep in your heart,
You're a rose, trampled into dust.

Cast aside, another deserted bride,
Mere chattel of narcissist love,
Walk away, slam the door

Future unknown, but you will survive
Because you
Are not afraid of tender love,
His ego will destroy him.

Once he is cast aside,
A worn out trophy, himself
He can't survive, cannot work at
Loving anyone, he is too selfish.

Believing that,
Tender love shall
Once again be yours
Can sustain you.
Until then, you know,
In your heart, you tried.

Ireland's Warriors

Let us
Dance, entwined.
Hold me close,
For your love is all.
In your eyes I see love
Though, I know it's not for me.
Your mistress, Ireland,
Has forever ensnared your heart.
That cruel Rosaleen.
On this night of sadness,
Please, hold me tight, let me
Kiss your mistress' eyes.
I know your thoughts,
Lie with her, and tomorrow
Shall be a blood filled day.

Homewards

How about we head homewards,
See if any of the
Old haunts exist today?
Perhaps they will feel
Colder, than on
Our yesterdays,
What's your fancy, going?
Homewards, and
See if we would feel part of?

Look at the faces
Peering from old, new
New net curtains, let's go home, and stand
Around as we did when
We were kids;
Remember those
Long summer nights, hopefully
Those old, childish streets will welcome us,

They might not even be
There, torn down, rebuilt, into
A modern slum, hope not, want
The memories to be alive,
One time neighbours to say hi, are you
Staying awhile, it would be sad
To be a stranger in the town
 We went to school in.

Now we're here, and leaning once more
Up against, the lamp post.
Who's that waving over there?
Why, it's Shelia,
Though might not be.

That old dear's got grey hair
Though, come to think
Of it, so have we.
How things have changed, let's
Jump a plane out, go home?
Last time we left, couldn't
Afford the bus, old time's
Best left behind.

Do Nothing

What can I do, what can I say,
Nothing, I can say.
Nothing I can do, wring my hands.
Weep tears of hot regret.
What use tears as, Palestine dies?

Nothing I can say nothing I can do,
Or undo Israeli troops kill, again,
And again nothing I can do,
Nothing I can say shall change things.
Israel has carte Blanche must be alright
Barack, Brown agree, they say nothing,
There's nothing I can do, carry on .

Weeping tears of indifference,
Israeli bombs, and Hamas
Rockets maim, and kill the innocent.
What can I do, what can I say,
Can I not win by ballot box?
Watch Israel defeated by world's abhorrence.

That is what we can do, that is how we
Do something, no longer stand back
In cold indifference to a nation's plight.
It's Palestine's right to live on the land,
Their land that Israel annexed.

Lifelines stretching back
Into centuries ago.
How far back do we need to go
To begin telling the tale,
19th century is remote enough,
The famine years
Of 1846 in Ireland.
Land of my ancestors that's
The moment in time,
My grandparents were born.

Another moment in time 1965
Teenagers meeting.

In a dance hall in Belfast town
Grandly name, the Astor.
Asking Geraldine
May I have this dance?
Innocent phrasing,

Strolling homewards later,
Then those fateful words -
May I see you again?
That moment in time
Creating another timeline

Karen, Joanne, Emma.

Lineage bestowed by those few words,
May I see you again?
Never once regretted
Though war often declared,
Then grandchildren arrived
First Christian, then Jordan
Amber, Trey, Caedon, Marcus.

Now a flower has bloomed
In Australia called Lilyana, yet
Another lifeline bestowed in a land
Far from ancestral homelands.
Lifetimes, and lifelines, flow onwards
The mists of time
An endless streaming.

Love you all, your granddad John.

It's early morning, and I'm staring
At a tree, seemly slouching against the
Early morning mist, and I think.

Unlike the corner boy who
Never thinks, only reacts.
That the tree will blossom gracefully,
As sunlight chases away,
The mist. The corner boy
Slouching, with hands in pockets

Shall, never offer the shelter
That the tree provides. With deep
Brooding eyes he gazes, balefully
Upon the world.

Nature nurtures, the corner boy destroys.
One wonders, shall he ever stand erect.
Stare straight and true, provide shelter,
And protection to his young?

The slouch says it all, "I don't care".
The tree, and I care, we need to declare
The days of indifference are over.
We all must provide care and shelter.

Resources

Road or rail, sea and sky
Movement of goods
Never cease
Fossil fuels wasted
Though goods will move
By road or rail, sea and sky
Resources gone, depleted.
But goods must move
By road or rail sea, and sky
Feeding the stomach of avarice.

On Angels' Wings

Not only angels can fly so high.
Reach out, reach out your hand
And help a friend along on life's
Arduous trails, we can all be angels.

Forget yourself, reach out and soar,
No fear, only caring and sharing,
Loving and comforting each other
On these lonesome trails of living, no one
Can stop you, if you just let go, and let God in.

No blame game, only loving and caring,
Reach out your hand, do it today.
Let's all soar on angels' wings

Poor man, rich man, beggar man or thief.
We are all God's children, we can all be
Angels, simply reach out your hand
And soar. Let's all be angels, for one day.

Adversity of Vanity

I need, I need
What I need
This and that
When I get what I need
Will I be content with my lot?

No, I still need
What is it you need?
How do I know, I just want
When I have it, I shall be content
Perhaps, well, maybe.

Why have I gotten to this state of wretchedness?
Needing, always wanting
And never content
He has, she has, and they have
What, I don't know
I just want more.

Style, more homes
More men and women
I need it all
Whatever all implies
Having it all, and being content.

Now there lies the crux of vanity
I created this state of adversity
Because I want it all.

Those people who have nothing
I perceive them as having more than I do
And they have love, contentment, and compassion.

Honour in their souls
That is what I truly need
But do I want it? No!
Why not?
Because I would have to do without all my possessions.

Die Sighing

It seems only yesterday that the poppies
Blushed crimson in Flanders fields.
Yesterday is our today although, in this dust
And stone of Afghanistan if a poppy
Could be found its colour would reflect
Embarrassment at our politicians allowing
Young soldiers to die in another useless war.

"We the people" should not let apathy sway
Our condemnation of fickle smug, and for one
Family of so called presidents, their pride
Betray us into saying that was yesterday.

Far too many body bags pile up.
We cannot forget they contain the
Bodies of our young: men, and women.
Brought back from what is today our Flanders,
Dunkirk, the Tet offensive, Iraq, their vainglorious
Deaths whispered about by politicians.

How many of their young people went to fight
For God, and country. Not many, I expect, though
They want you, to fade away as they murmur lies
That it is needed. We know they feign
To listen to our plea - end it now, save our young!

Instead, telling "we the people"
It is needed for "God and country"
Let us ask Obama which God,
What country, we are the country.
The good of the people is the chief law,
Why won't politicians
Listen to our young as they die sighing?

Never Did

Why did I not, get to know you?
Never stopped longer than to
Say hello, is he ready to go?

Just there to drive him, to work.
Never stopped to ask you a question.
Always walked away, never looking back.
Hadn't thought about falling in love after all,
You and me, such old time friends.

Quite simply, never knew you.
Even when I was with you,
Never realized you were only you and I
Used to people being other people
Never took the time to know you.
Sadly you passed away,
Now I cannot drive away, or say hello.
Too late, I'm wonderfully trapped
In loving you, time is so finite.
We forget, only a short span is allowed,
And it is but a moment from cradle to the grave.

In loving memory of wee Lizzie Loughran of Scotch Street, the Pound Loney, Belfast.

Hung-over

Struggled onto a train.
Slumped into a seat.
Think it was a Monday,
Wasn't going anywhere.
Guessing the driver knew
We would end up somewhere.

Anyway, I was hung-over.
Going any place held more
Appeal than going nowhere.
Train moved off, as they are
Trained to do.
Glanced askance at my fellow
Travellers thinking, bloody hell.

They looked a lot worse than I felt.
Train slowed, lights changed to red,
Same colour as my eyes. And there
Sat I - in this carriage of early morning
Thinkers, me! I'm drinking, they're all
Moaning about their bosses, and getting sicker.

Opp's bloody light has turned green,
Same shade as my fellow travellers.
Holy God, now I'm really going somewhere,
Stuff it, think I'll get off at next stop, go to
The drinking club, in the morning I won't
Be worried about my carriage inmates, they're
The people in a hurry, I'll just be hung-over.
Struggle onto a train going anywhere?

Bag of Hammers

I've been given a bag of hammers
Pondered on where to use them
While pondering I thought I'll knock some sense into people
Looked around
Who shall I start with?

Then looked at myself
Good beginning, I need a thump
When I finished with myself, I left bloodied and bewildered, no wiser.
I thought it would be easier to talk with someone,
I'll go out.

Leave my bag of hammers behind,
Striking out doesn't work
Find a friend, shake their hand
Walk with them awhile, talk with them,
It might work in an easier, softer way.

Talking Love

Let's talk about love.
Enchantment of the heart,
Beauty told and untold.

Stop a moment, watch
As it unfolds, natural acts
Of simplicity, discovered
Only in a loved one, and another.

Hold each other
Kiss one another
Dance with each other
Caress, hug, and kiss.
Let's talk about love.

Many romances are lost
In untold moments of
Charades of loving.

Touch gently, lightly
Upon bodies in love,
Whisper loudly, shout
I love you.

Forever in love as you
Soar together
Throughout endless days.

Moments of beauty stretch
Into eternity, scented thinking,
Fall in love talking love.

Fearful

Silently, the owl swoops
Catches its prey, soars skywards
To alight upon the eyrie where
It devours its kill, hunting only to live.
In it's world, nature's preserve, survival.

Why does humanity hunt? No need to kill.
Old and infirm their specialty, no threat
To their masculinity, only reward fear.
Elderly trying to survive in this inexplicable
World of hate, learn debilitating fear.

Once again thugs win, elderly huddle
Together, fearful, all vestige of humanity
Swept aside in bewilderment, lost in a prison
Of indifference built by the silent majority.
Their joy in living - shattered.

Locked in fortress blocks of concrete
Imprisoned by the fear of the crime,
Tired and weary they should be allowed
To smile after life's travails, humbled they
Only ask on bended knees, please help me.

Silence

Did you say something?
A week from last you spoke.
What!!!
Did you speak?
A gestures speaks,
Eloquent thoughts
Of unspoken dreams.
Pardon, you spoke?
Maybe I'm not listening.
Silence grips my mind until
Creaks, groans, hammer sounds
Become the silent speech of life.

When You Were a Young Girl

Hi there, I remember when you
Was a girl, going your own winsome
Ways, little did we know the many trails,
The many tales you would one day tell.
About lands you visited, wondrous sights,

The many glorious, delight filled nights,
Fond memories stored lovingly within
Your heart. Wanderings finished, change
Has arrived. Grandchildren around you
And the tales you tell enchant them all.
Many sights mysteriously conjured to
Delight and cause fright.

One day in future times they shall sit,
After youth is over, they will recount
About many trails and many tales
They ventured along. And you knowing
All those trails lead back to where you started.

You're roving over, you sit contented, that
Winsome smile dancing in your eyes.
And I, remembering when you were a girl,
Know why I always loved you, Gerry.

Losing You

I'm bleeding tears in my heart,
That secret place
Shared only with you,
Your love dared to enter,
And I was ensnared forever.

You became no
Stranger to my heart,
I knew I could believe in you.
Lord knows it will be sad
Walking all alone.

The hard face, the calm face,
That accepting face shown to
This world, only you know of
The tears I bleed for you,
And only you ever knew the true me.

The heartbreak in my heart
Reminds me of my mourning.
In time the tears
Will cease to flow,
But my memories of you
Shall be forever carried
On the wind, when I feel it blow.

As I hold your hand,
And you slip away, I accept that
Among the stars at night
All I need do is breath a quiet hello.
Be at peace knowing, you are there,
And I can be still.

Madness of Customers

Patiently waiting on customers,
Listening to drivel, dribbling out of puerile
Mouths. Wondering what they are saying.
Trying to make sense out of utter nonsense.

Spending the majority of work-time, lifetime,
Listening, agreeing, pricing.
An endless charade of drivel, from me
As I pay obeisance to their garbage.
Every day wasted in being utterly polite.

Wondering all the while under that polite exterior
If I garrotte him, her, perhaps, maybe, certainly,
I shall get away with it, that's when you realise
Their drivel, dribbling is driving you insane.
Your normal insanity rising up to greet their madness.

Have to go somewhere, anywhere
That impatience is not tolerated.
The moon seems good, might be
Far enough away to escape mankind's drivelling.

Redemption Road

Can peace be found in redemption?
It's always the road least travelled.
We enjoyed living life
On the road of perdition.

Savouring the forbidden fruits, believing
We are Jack the lad, one of the damned.
Though once that cell door slams shut
Then we find out if, having done the crime,
Let's see if we can do the time.

That's when the mind starts running down
The freedom road, no more Jack the lad,
On your own, thinking of redemption,
Peace of mind, that elusive concept you
Always abhorred in other folk, easier to sneer.

Now the dogs of war have drawn blood.
Snapping, yapping at your heels, nowhere
To run, the perdition road has brought
You low, can you find the redemption road
By reflecting on past hurts and crimes?
After all, time is the only ally you have.

Playing in the Dust

Another child dies, does anyone care?
Seven years of madness coming to an end?
Dust filled lane ways lined in death. Sorrowful
Playgrounds of today scream out their despair.

Will they remain our future when,
The greatest show on earth departs?
Seven years of playing in the dust of
Our Iraqi homeland as American troops
Surged through, killing our fathers, brothers,
Sisters, and mothers - Obama's playgrounds
Belies his truth of "Secondary troops"...

He proclaims
His righteous wish to play only a secondary
Part in our playground of dust saying, I have
Got the ball, it's mine, and I'm keeping it.
We will never see our homeland set free.

50,000 combatants playing with their eye
On the ball as it bounces between
Afghanistan, Iran, Iraq, and we the children who
Own the ball left to play in another
American dust bowl of lies and perfidy.

Useless Mutterings

I'm sitting here in this comfortable armchair
Drinking, and doing some mutterings about the
State of the world. It's easy thinking watching
The news as one is drinking, to expound
Your views about the disasters here and there
Around the world, not that I care I'm drinking.

Give the odd shout of remorse
Shudder amidst your mutterings but don't
Ask me to help rebuild a structure. I'm here
Doing nothing, only drinking and saying
How awful those poor people.
My platitudes easing my conscience knowing
I don't really give a damn.

I'm just drinking, and doing some useless
Easy thinking as I put on another sad song
Singing my slurred way through
The lyrics, and at the end of each useless
Verse congratulating myself on my selflessness.
Thinking, when I'm drinking, I really care.

One World

One single moment in time our
World stood still, and then
Little Boy, drifting in free flight
Caught the early Morning light, and
Stained our world with darkness.

Why did men carry in the wombs of
Their minds such total insanity
That "they" let Little Boy fall,
One wonders did they laugh or did
The closing of a city's eyes cause
Them any remorse? Answer must be no.
"They" let go of big boy's hand.

And then we have "they" who are they? (Politicians)
Who declared it would win a war.
Elected "by the people" did they tell
The people we have just destroyed
Twin cities of dreams to achieve victory?
One world, one race, the human race
Carried out this terrorist act.

Did they close their eyes against the flash
As the innocents ceased to exist?
Did "they" sift the ashes of Hiroshima and
Nagasaki? One world, our world must ask
Future generations was the price worth
That enduring shadow on the wall?
The Manhattan Project has laid waste to one world.

Four Dollar Man

I'm a four dollar man,
No more, no less, the worries I got are only
Four dollars worth.
That's why here,
In this hundred dollar land of way too much
I'm walking along on easy street.

No emptiness in my life, I smile every day.
Guess that's why I feel free, no worries
When you're a four dollar man, not working
Or getting into debt, knowing this day will pass away
Whilst I stroll along humming a song.
Watching the crowds stream around me, some scowling
Others worried. Not me, I'm the four dollar man.

One of these days some smart guy is gonna ask
How come you're always smiling? Won't believe my reason.

Because I'm the four dollar man, every day
Is a sunny day, reason the sun always shines
Is because I believe in God's love, and whilst I'm only
A four dollar man I've got a good guy walking alongside me.
His love makes me smile every day, knowing he will provide.

Here and Now

Here and now
Thinking about the folly of
Youthful indiscretion
Did we really believe
We were invincible then?
Now, in these so called
Golden years of greyness,
All the mistakes made and
Not a lot achieved.
Guess we accept the adage -
We did the best we could.

No gain in saying - should have, maybe if...
Point is: didn't.
Here and now, only time that matters
Can't afford any if's, or should have's,
No time left, just use today's reality.

We are upright, and on the ground, not below it.
Easier to accept old time dreams and lovers lost
Along the many trails, letting our grievances
Lie in the dust whilst we talk, talk,
Sharing memories in the here and now.

They Were Kids

They remain kids, we sent them off
To war-torn lands, and when they returned
We, the adults, buried them deep in the grounds of
Their childhood towns, and there they remain. Always kids.
In this our world, peace is deemed an absurdity - *Why?*

We judge, we condemn, we destroy all, and everyone
Who will not think as we do, do as we do, kill as we do.
Who are we? We are the people of all nations under God
Call him by any name you wish, *Thou Shalt Not Kill* is
A commandment of all the entities we care to name.
Why then if we call upon God are we still burying the kids deep?
In the cold, cold ground, instead of nurturing them.

When I condemn you, you, you, I am pointing at myself.
I am to blame because I am you, the destroyer of innocent kids.
It's easy this killing, we let our elected representative call the shots.
Decide who we should let our kids kill, and then when our kids are dead
We can condemn those people who sent them off to war-torn lands.
After all it was not "we the people", can't blame us, you our politician killed our kids.
We disguise ourselves as responsible adults, and we bury the kids.

Resentment

Last night I met an old friend who,
Strangely enough, greeted me in an affably way.
Now, this same guy I had carried ill thoughts for many a day.
Being that insincere man
I said hello, and talked for awhile.
You know, whilst we talked
The resentment I bore him went away.

Simple reason
I couldn't remember what had annoyed me
To avoid such a gentle guy, all these years.
It now seems strange that all that bitterness and hurt
Was a wasted effort. All it did was made me a very unlikeable guy.
I took down his mobile, and of course he took mine
It will be strange, but nice, to be in touch again after all this time.

I went on my way trying to remember my resentment
Then thought, what's it matter, you are both friends again.
Though in all truth it was only me, carrying an imagined slight
That drove a wedge between me and such a guy.
All it needs to destroy a friendship is silence, and resentment.

The Brow of the Hill

Climb that hill, stand gazing at endless housing
All that can be seen, but open your mind, and
Gaze with fresh eyes, you can, and will see beyond
The horizon, endless sights just there in your mind,
Only reason there are endless housing is because you
Don't open your heart and see beyond these city walls.

If you climb to the brow of the hill, take my advice, open
Your mind, your heart, and all the joy of endless delights
Fill your soul with wondrous light, country, or city, once
There on the brow of the hill with a closed mind nothing
Has any meaning, it's all trite, reason why you may have
Climbed the hill but can't see beyond the horizon. You're
Only climbing, yearning, and hoping for a little bit of faith.

Once you're on the brow of the hill your heart will open.
And all will become clear, you have conquered all your fears,
Let your mind roam beyond the City walls, look upon
Your world and laugh out loud, on the brow of the hill
All is possible if you open your soul and embrace your world.
The long climb is over, you are on the top of the world.

I Cannot Weep for America

I cannot weep any tears of remorse for America,
They have stolen, and raped carte-blanche throughout
Our world of emerging economies, now they stand
With their sword of Damocles hanging, whilst wily
Politicians twist and turn that delicate thread creating
With sleight of hand the illusion of China, Asia, taking all
From the ordinary Joe of America, not letting on that
Their self-seeking capitalists are reaping the benefits.

Those golden years when all was good, and spend, spend, spend
Was the order of the day, waste - no such word, throw it away,
Get another, another what, who cares just spend,
It helps the economy, people starving overseas not our problem,
We are America, land of the free, and now we are free,
Free to endure poverty at 43 percent of our spend, spend economy,
The government talks about the now, the stimulus, stumbling
Around trying to fashion a new deal, there is no new deal in sight.

Our manufacturing industries such as Dell, need we ask why it
Invested 100 billion in China leaving behind any thought of America?
After all, "profit" that's the bottom line in American speak, not piety
Or love of country; don't speak nonsense, honour, God and America,
Leave that to the masses, it's a euphemism part of the sleight of hand
To confuse and deceive, if you the people want your country back
Look to your past, remember you do not need to beseech or wring
Your hands, plead, and cringe. Stop! Demand, protest, before your politicians sell
A M E R I C A.

Lilyana

A child is born today, Lilyana
Is her name, she entered
Our world without a cry looking
Beautiful, smooth as a soft rose petal.

Gently held by her mother
Who bore her so bravely,
Her eyes wide open, you would
Believe she new all that was going on.
Cameras flashing, she ignored them -
Feed me, hold me, and lay me down.
Lilyana gently took over her parent's world.

Weighting in at seven pounds, five ounces, and
Twenty inches in length the joy of her filled
That room with newborn life.
Nothing can ever be the same
Lilyana shall grow into a
Beautiful rose.

Since that one moment in time
When she fluttered as a petal into life
Her mum and dad's life changed.
Holding her in their arms,
Falling in love with their
Wonderful newborn baby called - Lilyana.

Your grandad John and nana Gerry
Wish you a long and happy life.

Xxxxxxxooooooo...
May God keep you and bless you always,
Lilyana.

The Man at the Door

Wait a moment, it's only a man at the door.
Has he got a notebook in his hand? Yes.
Why would it instil such fear in you?
Because he's here for money I don't have.
You're kidding, I thought you worked two jobs.

I do, but two jobs don't make any difference.
In this plastic society we pay the interest, and still
We cannot make enough to pay the man at the door.
It's his notebook I fear, all my rent arrears stored in there.
The child and I shall have to get out of here, can't pay my way.
Man at the door only doing his job, it's self seeking landlords
Between them and the plastic bankers we live in fear.

Our life today is to work, work and pay, we live in penury.
Working class of today have no champions to defend them.
The governments took our unions, the manufactures took our jobs.
And we, the people stand back whilst the man at door knocks away,
The stepping stones that made up our life, home and country sold
To the East, they too will become shredded people
That one day shall have to fear
The man at the door.

Lights Out

Is this all we can do? Stand and watch as
The lights grow dim, who can we blame?
Who threw the switch and manipulated it that the
Western world would grow dark one day, one month
At a time? Now we see in the dusk all the factories are gone.

Nothing left to live on, only dust in our lives.
But "they" say pay your mortgage, pay your rent. We need
To demand - switch on the lights and take back the work,
Living in darkness created by big moneyed corporations.
"They", who with malice threw the switch and watched without
Care as our lives run into utter despair yet deny we ask
Any remit on their decision to throw the switch,
Demand we stand quietly aside with begging bowl in hand,
Suppliants pleading - have mercy.

They have us on our knees, we must rise, ask why the
Switch was thrown on the Western dream. Is it because
Those with plenty, cast greedy eyes on beleaguered people
Further east and sought larger profits, haven't enough in their
Coffers? We can only watch in despair thinking when will
They throw the switch on the many varied people of the East.
Then, without regret turn out the light
And plunge our world into a long dark night.

Paint Me a Dream

What right has man to judge, and stone
A woman to death? Such bad behaviour
She expressed, improperly dressed,
And with, horror of horrors, talking
With a man not related. The Mullahs
Don't want women to be angels, just good slaves.

Wear your niqaab, stay at home, and don't answer back.
You are inferior. The fundamentalists paint a picture
Of nightmares against women who live in a dream.
Thinking they are equal, should be treated with respect.
Then time after time shown they are lesser than a man.
Cannot make a decision not allowed to participate in social or
Political debates, stay at home remember your gender. "Inferior!"

Paint me a dream of respect. Answer me - why can we not make
Family decisions, have custody of our children, work where we
Decide, not you, it's time we rose and demanded our equality.
Give us our humanity, let's find a way to be part of you, weave a weft
Of "a people" dressed and living as we desire.
Paint me a dream, one where the stoning of
Sakineh Mohammadi-Ashtiani cannot, and will not happen.

Frozen Words

Words heard to echo
Throughout the night
Disappear in the bright
Light of day, frozen now,
Their import lost forever
All I can do is rise up, get
Dressed, and regret the lost words.
Left to dissolve in a warm bed.

No chance to recall all or
Anything that the subconscious
Thought so wise in the dark of the night.
I will sit and think throughout the day
Trying to remember the brilliant poem
I wrote in my mind during the long dark night,
Lost now in daylight, wondering was it love,
Or lust, hopefully it was about the beauty of loving.

I can only sit now, and think of love.
Frozen forever, knowing it as a love that will
Last, that never ending beauty captured
In soft morning daylight never fearing it to
Be consumed by other frozen words.

Random Man

Wandering through this repressed land
I find myself living as a random man -
No place worth stopping, no place
Worth going to, just another
Rolling stone trying to survive
On life's lengthy highway.

Looking into garbage bags
Grab hold of a can, don't let go, it's all
This random man has, other people's
Food in this lost land, used to be
A worthwhile man then the bankers
Changed our lives stripped us of all we had
Now I wander, no home, no hearth.

I hear the clamour of voices at night
Claiming it'll be alright though I
Can't see an end in sight, believe I will
End up as a wandering random man.
Only thing I have left is to be the best I can.

Aussie Made

Ten more years in Afghanistan? we exclaim,
Why, we won't, can't accept another ten.
Ms Gillard says I shall explain -
We have to support our allies
Now. Ms Gillard isn't heard saying
Though they, like us, are corrupt.

And we, Aussies, accept without
Protest this claim of necessity
To let another ten years of attrition
Flow past, defending a land that is alien.
It's time to ask - please explain without
Double speak the why of it all, 21 of our young
Men lost to uphold this most heinous war.
We, the Australian people, are not wrong, we listen
With minds tired of rhetoric, complaisance. You ask
Be strong and let you carry on.

In ten more years how many of our young
Shall lie dead in this war of exhaustion,
Now is the time for all to exclaim no!
Desist or we shall resist, protests on the streets
Reclaim our young soldiers' lives.
Have you no shame, this war is not Aussie made?
We cannot stay another ten years.

Climb down from the podium, Ms Gillard, climb
Into a bushmaster then say yes, another ten is needed.
Go on patrol, fear the roadside bomb, sniper fire,
Then come back to camp, and state fear not another ten.
And we shall be gone, what then Ms Gillard will our
Allies be where we truly belong,
In the east, the west long gone.

And Now - A Word from Brian

Old glory calling me home.
No choice, had to go -You called, Lord.
Here I am, unwillingly, wish you had let me
Bid my friends goodbye. They'll think it strange
Not hearing my chuckling, ah well, when those trumpets blow
Got no choice, we gotta go.

Follow that sound, I hear my wife Maggie crying aloud
Brian, Brian, my childer, and granchilder,
They cry out to me, whilst here I lie casket bound
Can't reach out to reassure them I'm okay,
Heard the sound of glories horn, I'll go,
Look around, judge for myself the truth of eternity.
Old glories trumpeters have blown the gates wide open,
    letting me see were I'm bound.

Don't worry about me, I'll be around.
Now if you would all hush awhile - listen to my chuckle,
Say a quiet prayer, it'll help me on my way.
Maggie will say Brian's still here though,
When she looks around it causes a tear to fall,
Brian's not in his usual chair.
Glory called, I've no choice, gotta go -
Old Glory's called me home.
Quietly I go, and leave you with this thought:
    I love you, one and all

This is written about my big brother Brian who died suddenly on the 29th of October. Maggie is his wife of 50 years - he will be sorely missed. If anyone had a problem and asked him for help, they heard that immortal phrase of his: "Na bother". They knew all would be sorted out by Brian. My Big Brother.

Grey Men

Gaunt and haggard they stand on every corner
Of Old Belfast Town, these grey, faceless men.
Hiding from the light, lurking in shadows,
Watching for the main chance, they will
Take your life, your soul, your dignity.

Cloth caps pulled low to shield their hooded eyes
Watching, always watching, taking all, giving nothing
Except mayhem - no remorse, no regrets,
Selfish gain, all they ever do is inflict pain.

Good folk struck down, prey to the Grey men.
See them shuffle up and down peering furtively
Around Town, waiting, always ready to strike
The average Joe trying to do what is right,
Eight to four his working plight whilst the Grey men,
Chameleon like, wait to strike.

All you have, all you earn is fodder for their
Material gain, standing on street corners, scheming
To take, they never care when they bring you down,
Why do we let them stand around? Our fault, tolerating
Grey, faceless, characterless men in any Town.

And All That There

Went into the house the other day
Talking to em in ere and all that there
And like it was as if I wasn't really
There know wot I mean, like
I didn't exist or summit
Me standing there like a dummy
And all that ther pissed of I was
Know waw I mean might as well
Have left they didn see me one of them
Said hello an all that ter but I just left
No wot I mean like it was all that there.

Now if all that there is perfectly clear to
All who read it good luck because it's a load.
Of all that there, know what I mean like.

Thanks to You

Thanks to you - I am
Thanks to you - I understand.
Thanks to you - I became a man.
Thanks to you - love is a gift.
Thanks to you - I can cope with hardship.

Thanks to you - you are my world.
Thanks to you - I have compassion.
Thanks to you - I sing, and dance.
Thanks to you - I can be myself.
Thanks to you - our children grew.
Thanks to you - my world is complete.
Thanks to you - who would love me?
Thanks to you - I'm complete.
All that remains to say is - I love you.
Let me hold you - and thank you.
Thanks to you. You are woman.

This Place

We all begin the same and all
End up at the same destination - dying.
This place where we are journeying through
Is called life, how we react
To events along the way decides
If our journey is worthwhile,
Decisions made and acted upon
All have consequences

This tale of living has to include
The one constant in life's travels
From this place where we started,
Its called love - to be loved,
And to be in love. We cannot
Stand back ever and state
We have never been in love

Love is a state of being you,
Me, us, and them, the human race.
This place where we all started from
Loving, it starts before our eyes,
Twirls us around then either holds on
Tightly or spins off into eternity.

Leaving us to decide, did we know
From whence we started?
I don't think any of us ever know,
Though this place where
It all started is a wonderment of life.
One which the only understanding is
There is No understanding.

Let's travel onwards
Towards our ending, being

The very best we can be
At living, and loving.
This place where we all start
Is called - Humanity's journey.

Hobby Horse

When I was but a child
I played on the hobby horses,
Usually on mild sunny days.

Days of innocence that have now run their course,
Local Bobbies chased you for playing ball
Never for running and shouting yourself hoarse.

Shouts of glee and merriment as we spun
Above the ground on our carousel of gold,
Of course we all felt so very, very bold

Playing on the hobby horses, not knowing
Or showing fear, after all we were kids
When our mothers called we let on we didn't hear.

The clip-clopping of the old horse was greeted
With the swelling of children laughing and playing
Only memories remains of hobby horses going round

Along with the local Bobbies chasing children.
No one to lobby for the hobby horses, they died away
And left a deep cleft in the streets of Belfast town.
Who would ever have thought the hobby horse would die?

Computer Deaths

What is guilt, when fingers war on people,
Bloody conflict unseen
Only depicted on screen,
Where is war, it's only another movie?

Twisted lives, ruined cities, people screaming
Let the mouse roam free
Your fingers play at war
No maimed or legless heroes -
You are deep in bunkers
Shielded from reality.

Let your fingers dance macabre
Across your console,
What consolation is there
For the millions of dead?
Its governments' bloodless war.

Buried deep in computer, living
People, families, roaming on
Your screen, are they not refugees
Fleeing your consequences?

NO! simply images, can fingers walking
On velvet green feel remorse
For people dying screaming?
Where is the compassion for death
Unseen when only your fingers do
The walking, no blood on your hands?

Happiness

All our tomorrows are memories to share
In companionship.
With love in our hearts
And compassion in your minds
You can soar
Through each new day.
That morning, awaking
Beside love's partner reassures you
About life's raptures,
Intimately surrendering
To one another it lets
Loves wonderment reflect
Upon our oneness of each other.
Sitting happily, drinking a coffee
As the morning dawn
Embraces us we can sigh peacefully
Knowing in our
Hearts - we love each other.

Tomorrows

All our tomorrows are memories
We should have shared,
Lifetimes that could have been.
We can never reflect on, those whispering
Caresses of love are gone.
But your memory is cherished forever in my soul.
Where you are in that silent land is unknown.
Though, having you in my soul I know that
One day we will soar together again.
Then we shall have memories to share.
Once again our loving dreams will envelope us
Letting us touch happily upon one another.
And into our future tomorrows we will soar.

Telling

What tales I could tell
If I didn't stop and think,
It would only be treading
Harshly upon your dreams.
After all I know they are.
All you have left to sustain you,
Those dreams of long ago
When life was great and anything
And everything was possible.
Those yesterday times when
You strolled and spoke of tomorrow.
Now all the tomorrows are passed
And your dreams lie in ruins.
When the cold winds of fate swept
Through your life leaving you helpless
Upon a bed of might-have-been,
That nothing phrase reverberating
In your mind - if only.
The tales I could tell are best left
To dreaming, knowing they are all
You have left to sustain you.

Rage

Fire in the mind
Rage in your heart
Death in your soul
Down, down, deep
With death's insanity
Lying down in gutters
With no peace in your heart
Embracing pain, asking God
To let compassion into your mind
All I can think is burn it all,
Burn it all, let the fire in my mind
Create a holocaust of peace in my heart.

Legacy

There were places I walked,
Left footprints behind,
Though some places I arrived at
No sign that I was ever there.
Perhaps others noticed an imprint.
I should have paid attention to time's swift passing.
The footprints I could have left might have given
Reason to living, instead, playing games with life
I didn't understand God's got his own plan.
None I would ever understand.
I simply lived life as it came at me.
Nothing to lose or, so I thought,
It's all been decided,
Part of God's grand plan though.
I should have reached out my hand,
Helped another soul along even if
They were not going my way.
Then any footprints I left behind
Would have been defined
In people's minds,
Cruising always in their hearts.
I should have known God's got his plan.
It might have helped if I had remembered
It's his master plan not mine.

Pair of Socks

Well, there was this pair of socks,
Actually they were a dirty pair of socks,
Dirty! Filthy would be a better description.
Anyway, there they were in innocent,
Mouldering slumber until some eejit
Asked why they were sleeping on the chair.
Seemed a logical place to me.

Strangely others didn't think so, anyway,
Under great duress to the socks I awoke them
Put them in the machine, you may ask what
Sort of machine? A washing machine, is there
Any other sort of machine for a dirty, smelly,
Slumbering pair of sock? No!

I didn't think so. Of course there is the bin.
Though, maybe I should have asked them, the socks
That is, to crawl under the chair. After all, they
Had been living there. You may ask yourself
Where this tale of the socks is heading. I haven't
Got a clue, maybe I should have just asked the socks -
Were they happy living on the chair?
And not listened to a couple of eejits in the first place.

Can't

You think you are standing still, you
Think you are sitting down,
Then why

Are you pacing around?
You think you are lying down

You think you are sleeping
Faces are crowding in
You think you are still,
You are always moving around

Images are fading,
Disappearing, appearing
Stop pacing - lie down
Stand still - sit down...

Can't!

Journeying

I'm on the train to anywhere,
Unconcerned about destination

Listening to the weighty thrum of
Wheels on steel, going anywhere

I'm heading outwards glancing
At nowhere towns wondering why

People needed to arrive, to belong,
Guess they may as well stop somewhere

On this crazy ride I will have endless
Charades of conversations unconcerned about nuances

After all I'm journeying on to anywhere
Where I boarded the train that was a destination

Now a memory shunted onto dead end line
Sharing thoughts with passengers, pointless

Why remember sad, bad, or good times
We're all journeying on the train to anywhere

If

If you are fortunate enough
To find true love in your lifetime
Then you shall live for all eternity.
If you do right, all that you are and
All that you do shall be remembered
With love, thus you are eternal.
The greatest wonderment in life is to love.
The greatest grief can come from that love.
But love never dies, only peoples die, their
Essence is forever, love's spirit can
Carry all of us onwards and upwards.
True love is a gift, treasure it always.

Dancing, with Lies

Dance me a dance, embrace me gently,
Swirl me around, go on, and dance me a dance,
Let's forget the old used to be, just sway with me,
Stay with me, twirl me lightly around, tell me you
Love me, even if it is a lie.

Dance me a dance, forget about tomorrows
We have only tonight, and the music.
Love me tonight, and don't think about our yesterdays.
Holding you tightly in my arms I feel
As though I'm dancing the dance of life.
All thoughts of self cast aside, all I want is you.

Dance with me one more time, the music still playing
Why leave, please, glance back, don't let me stumble
Around, as you fade out of the light,
Dance back into my life and let me tell you - I love you.
Please, dance me a dance even though I know, it's a lie.

I will dance with the lie, all that I have left are
The memories of you, always in the dance hall of dreams.
As you walked away, I wished you
Would tell me a lie, and say I love you.

Dreams Are Not Enough

Action is the answer after we dream
Let's put those thoughts into reality

What can be better than achieving your dream
That moment when you realise you have done it

The dream is reality no longer a concept, it's real
And better still - it's yours, thumbing your nose
At all the lifetime scoffers calling you a dreamer

Only dreamers achieve, the drones only serve
Let's keep on dreaming a dream
And putting them into action

Dreams and actions go together, we should all
Be dreamers

Drinking

Once I Chanced Upon The Wind.
It swirled around and befuddled my mind.
Then I chanced upon the stars, and
Glancing at them I had another jar.
Drunk and damned I might be, but
I can still let life's passions engulf me.

Perspective

Perspective we hide from
Though always it drives nails into
Our souls, never reflecting upon
Forgotten beliefs, dreams and schemes,
We are just a people no more
No less than others.
Perspective is simply life's way of
Letting us bask in our own importance.
Never realising we are hiding from judgement.

Yesterday

Dreams and hopes stumble into
Empty rooms an endless void
Never fading from our consciousness.
You face each day as an empty room,
Tomorrow the enemy hides in endless
Corridors, opening each new day
Into another silent, empty room.
Thoughts and echoes
Change reality as I remember people
And seemly endless conversations in
This now empty room

Being Me

Wherever I am, wherever I end, this is me,
Born, St James at 13 the Drive Falls road,
Then the Murph, moved over to north
Then back to south Belfast
Went further south, Cork, then on to Great Southern land,
This is me.

The sum of all places I have lived,
Travelled back to north of Ireland
Antrim Town this time, then thought I would move
Back, to west Belfast,
Great Southern land next stop?
Probably, and perhaps
Travelling onward
This is me.

In all certainty?
Then who knows, I don't,
Though, one constant thought always remains
Given time I will settle
North, South, East, West... not sure about west, not me.
Wherever I am at,
The one in the corner
Talking about moving on
This is me.

Perhaps, I should settle in Great, Southern land
Though North, South, West Belfast
Shall always, beckon.
However I end, wherever I end
This is me.

Strolling

Stroll down the mall
Stare into the shop windows
Do not stop, your pockets are empty
Insincere greetings await you
Only stare and stroll
Watch people buying
Wishing you had money,
Without it you can
Only stroll and stare
Wishful thinking gets you
Through your day,
Stroll, peer upon those
Goods of avarice,
Wishful thinking
When pockets are empty.

Dance of Firs

Cheerful winds choreograph
Graceful firs as if they are dancers,
Swaying backwards
And forwards, nature's doing no wrong
Gracefully encouraged in
The soughing breeze,
The evening's fading sunlight,
An enchantress as it slips
Gently into night's embrace
Leaving its expression of love
Dancing in the soft moonlight.
Nature's beauty an enchantment
As it sways about in the nights
Magical mystery of life.
We can all share in nature's
Wonderment holding hands
And wandering amongst
This dance, we know we
Can rest easy with nature's joy.

Living and Hoping

We look at life everyday
Unaware we let it slip away

Life is like a carousel turning,
And dipping all around we lost the
Knack of playing at life, finding it mundane

Until one day we stopped aghast
Realising life had slipped from our grasp

As a thief in the night we stole, and stripped
Our hearts of beauty's light finding pain
Instead of gain

Simple gain - the stars at night, dawn's golden
Sunlight, diffusing city lights, we stopped looking
At life's beauties

Now trying to salvage ourselves and let
Love's beauty shine in our life,
Even raindrops shimmering on a blacktop,
Highways are a wondrous sight

White lines disappearing into a far distant horizon
Allow us to lift our eyes and gaze at God's magnificent
Creation, living after all is like a carousel

And we should ride it onwards as if once again
We are children playing at life, finding the
Pleasure we lost whilst working at living

Last Night

Late last night when I couldn't sleep
My thoughts drifted to you
I pictured you as a cloud casting your
Shadow upon the ground being pushed gently
By prevailing winds sweeping over undulating hills
My thoughts were only of you, and although
I didn't sleep I was content drifting alongside
Of you, in my thoughts we were together
Embracing in your cloud we gently passed
Time in a dreamscape late last night when
I couldn't sleep.

Tin Hat Days

told this by a girl who lived on the streets of London as a child, called them her tin hat days

It's another one of those black, black days
Either day or night nothing's going right

Just a tin hat day, keep my head down
And endure, try and forget the
Guys who ripped me off, took me on, promised all

Keep my tin hat well in place
It wards off all the blows
Physical and mental

Don't own anything, it's all in hock
To someone else, even my mind
Is not my own, gotta keep my tin hat on

I'll just wander around hoping my
Emotions won't get ripped apart
Each empty day looking for love

None to be found, simply putting my
Heart in hock for another day
Gazing at the ground after being used

Lucky I have my tin hat, don't think
I would be alive without it, hate these
Days of constant use, nowhere to live,
Find a quiet doorway and get some rest

Belfast, Two

Belfast is a killing town
Lying between heathered hills
Its charm worked on all who visited

Soft greetings in its splendid pubs
Belies its violence
Where faceless men parade as innocents
Our culpability lending a hand to their thoughtless motive

Hardness grips a once heathered town
Its bloom gone, only a sigh of madness whispers along these streets of welcome

Easy Thinking

It's easy to sleep on another
Man's wounds, you can live
In legends, die in folklore.
Never seeing or feeling the reality
Of pain, and bloody death.
Folklore is clean, sterile, gently
Laying down the book, so much
Easier than holding a dying comrade.
Or staunching the blood from your own wounds.
We can simply take on the platitudes of
Politicians, their lies are easier to absorb.
It's simpler than tending to another man's wounds.
You can talk, talk, about great deeds
Though you will never walk alongside heroic
Comrades, feel their sadness, their families' pain.
Folklore you lived through, never realising
Those legends are ordinary men and women
Refusing to accept the slights and wrongs
Of foreign merchants declaring their
Right to steal by government decree.
It's easier to sleep in another man's wounds.

Believe in the Soul, Two

Since you have gone you
Remain locked in my soul

Today, tonight, loving you
We will always be as one

When your loved one has gone
From this world their soul is steadfast

You are entwined as one. Believe
In the soul, it marches to a different beat

One we can neither see nor touch though
At times you feel its presence

Believe in the soul, in that simple
Belief there is the reward of great peace

You know your loved one is always there
To guide and protect you,
Believe in love, believe in the soul

Avarice

Empty hangers bring back the memories of love once cherished
Before it became lost in forests of fully draped hangars
Money inevitably dominated
Life became worthless
Only draped hangers prevailed

Thoughts of plenitude stroking the love once cherished
Large home, large car, small life
Hangers fully draped denote our slide into love lost
Open wardrobe door glimpse
Empty hangers a crescendo of silence

Smashes into life's imagined plenitude
Realizing life should have been full of love
Never draped on hangers covered with avarice
Falling for fool's gold glittering, beckoning,
Leaving only an empty life where love ha
Been lost to a forest of empty hangers

Cast a Long Shadow

Setting out on the long dusty road
Hoping we can end up casting a
Long shadow, not knowing where
We are going but smiling and being
Cheerful maybe, as time goes by
Helping strangers through the long

Lonely nights talking, laughing, not letting
Them think of the cold, cold rain knowing
As they shrug their shoulders
In the morning sunlight they will see you have
Cast a long shadow throughout the cold night

Find them somewhere to crash and eat
Will be better than out on the long dusty road
Maybe a change will take place if we smile
And find the sunshine has lengthened their shadow

All they need to do is hold on, and not take
Second best, they have the gift of life
And you know they are going to cast a long shadow

Never Alone

We're never alone if we talk to God
Hard to do when you don't believe
But always noticed those people who
Pray seemed never to be alone, as for me
I seem unable to find peace.

Maybe if I talk to God I'll not be alone
Can't do any harm to try, not getting
Anywhere being on my own, maybe the god bloke
Will say hello who knows, might as well try
At least I won't be alone on fear filled nights
Pain of living could be put right.

If we talk to the god fella
Even believe at the mention of his name
Hello God this is me, is that you, I'm trying
To believe hoping I'm not to late and end
Up only a number on your slate to be stroked off.
Be good never to be alone.

Was Thinking

I was thinking if truth
Be told, I would like to
Meet you again

Recall memories of
Past times good or bad
Just thinking of you

How about we meet again
Even one time, give you a hug
And tell you I've missed you

The time spent with you is
Still crystal clear even in a
Mind as dim as mine, though

You are easy to recall,
Yes I would like to meet
You again because in life every
Second counts

Let's meet and talk of old pledges,
Laugh at love won or lost, of people
We met along the way, let's do it,
Let's meet again

Knaves Laughing

Standing now at the abyss
Having heard all the lies
Telling us we can have it all
Those laughing times when the
Workers twirled thinking they had it all,

And didn't realise they were listening
To knaves laughing, telling them the price
Is right, £100,000, one million, one billion,
Grabbing at life we forgot
The price is rarely right.
Dust bowls of money blinding lives
We live in capitalist times not aware that

Mr Heep is squeezing our hearts telling us
Dance, twirl, it's all Big Brother lies.
Forgetting lockouts, handouts, lookout
It's happening, dust bowls of money blowing
In plain sight, look to your past there is no
New deal in sight only an eastern promise
And knaves called bankers
Laughing, and robbing our lives

Empty Arms

Here I'm standing with empty arms
The childer are all gone.
And I'm facing another lonesome day
'Tis strange listening to the noise
Of silent rooms.

The noise of love
Has faded away from my empty arms.
It's not that I'm complaining, ach,
Perhaps I am but listening to this
Silence is hard to bear

Since the childer
Were taken from me, and lord God, I
Would rather have my arms full again
With them all a squealing and a yelling.
Yet here I stand, with empty arms.

Reflections of a Woman

Quietly, joyful wee Liz enthralled everyone she met.
Her eyes, dancing in merriment, reflected the beauty
Of her mind where the trueness of humanity lies,
Whether just watching TV or drinking tea, wee Liz was
Always at peace - even with me.

She loved to talk, dance, though enjoyed the bingo more.
Was a quiet woman - never a complaint, smoked too much,
Didn't drink, and me being me I could not complain.
Learned to drive at age 48, of course - a natural,
Being a quiet woman,

Competent at all she did but another one of those ladies
From a generation of working class that never got a chance
To express her wonderful abilities fully.
All of her life she helped any one who asked, and those
Too shy or proud to ask for help - she was there to give advice.
Now, gone into the silent land at age 53, she left her wonderful
Presence behind, that singular. Quietly vibrant, beautiful woman -
wee Liz.

Peaceful Lady

A thug screams out of a mordant mind -
Do this, do that, are you stupid?...
Please, peaceful lady asks - what do you want?

Will you not help? a screams spews out
Of thug's sightless, blank mind. Do what?
He forms a fist, peaceful lady cringes.

Later he curls up against her, which he expects.
The complaisant body peaceful is cringing, fearful,
Then suddenly peaceful lady is full of rage

Thinking - if I rage he might harm the child.
I shall stay flexible, my God, who is
This thug I am married to,

Should I steal quietly away into the night,
Look for refuge, forget the broken promises?
Then thinks - I'm not a thief in the night,

He has always been, I shall walk proudly
Away, hold my head high, I'm the most important
Person not him. My child and I, we will survive.

Nothing

If you expect nothing
You'll get nothing
At least you'll still
Have nothing.
So you get what
You expect,
Precisely nothing.
So you have nothing.
Then maybe its
Better to expect nothing.

Lost in a Familiar Place

Looking around, watching
Normality
Thinking I should know this place
Knowing I recognize nothing.

Seeing familiar sights, realising
They aren't real, well not to me
Lost as I am in a familiar place.

I watch people fade in, fade out
Of my life
I never take the time to say hello,

Always moving on, never stopping
Long enough to acknowledge anyone,
Even the half seen wraiths drifting with me

Are old friends, older lovers all
Along for the ride, ending up
God knows where, lost in a familiar place.

A Life Well Lived

It is a long, lonely time
Since I have seen her smile
The smile I cherished
That spoke of love and caring.

Alas, today my lovely girl has lost her smile
That fickle road of life we stride has taken its toll.
As we all in youthful arrogance were invincible
She has arrived at fate's doleful door, and heard the bell toll.

It is a hard, hard time to smile
When you accept your moment of leaving has arrived
Though she states it gives her freedom to look backwards
And forwards at a life well lived.

Then, at that, she smiles and sheds a tear, not in regret
But in thanks for all those good times of love and peace
And the realization that she would change nothing.

Now close your eyes and smile with "a lady",
Remember her as she slips away into God's embrace
Knowing she left behind a legacy of a life well lived.

Heroin Nights

Needle plunging downwards,
Never able to live or be at peace
With anyone, even yourself.

Selfish promises, broken dreams,
Heroin nights are all that matter.
Closed doors, love-full needles,
Stumbling through empty rooms.

Love's promise plunged downward
In one chaotic act, living your dreams
As if realities in paintings come to life.

Doors crashing shut. Coldness creeping into
Your heroin love-filled night
Reminding you he, she, has fled, taken flight
Into life, leaving you slumped in a filthy armchair.

Plunging needle into arm on another lonely,
Sick, pain wracked night, thinking drug is love's
True promise. Forgetting that limbo lies
Between heaven, and hell.

You, you're dying, crying on
Life's last dark heroin-filled night.
Only pain dominates, and you think
Of self, wishing for one more fix
As the cold spectre of death beckons.

Echo Man

I will, I won't, yes I shall and no I won't,
Okay, then I'll scream and shout, listen to
My shouting you see I'm the echo man living
Here in no man's land, you must understand
That. No, listen, they all repeat themselves,

Repeat themselves, repeat themselves, oh well
Living here in repeat-land hoping if I say it
Often enough and listen to my echo bouncing
Around maybe I'll live free in repeat-land.

No, you won't, yes I shall, I'm the repeat man
Simply passing through echo-land listening to
The echo, doing the same as everyone, not hearing
What's spoken, after all if we listened we might truly
Hear, and no longer exist here in echo-land.

Maybe it would be better if I became the stuttering man,
Then everyone hangs on your every word, better than
Being the echo man, I shall go and think about it, scheme
A way to escape this maddening land. You never know,
I may leave behind the echo man, echo man, echo man...

Autumn Drumlins

Soft autumn sunlight
Drapes itself languidly
Across ancient drumlins,
Their antiquity brought
Gloriously alive in green and golden-brown tilled fields.

Autumn looks fearlessly
Towards winter's hard times
Meantime, we gaze peacefully
Upon their tranquil pastoral setting.
A wonderland shown through God's

Mysterious handiwork
Allows us to gaze contentedly
Upon glacial ice cooled land
As sunlight slides gently, peacefully from ancient drumlins
And evening embraces the night.
We can leave tomorrow's problems for tomorrow.

Abandoned

You deserved a better life, wee Liz.
The one you lived, you lived it well,
Unfortunately those who surrounded you
Were useless to the point of criminality.

I include myself in that truth.
You loved and cherished all your children,
You cared and shared with everyone you met,
Those who should of looked after you did not, they abandoned you.

You fought the fight of life to survive
For your children to grow up and live well,
You spent lonely nights wondering where the money
To pay bills was coming from.

The hero who married you tarried in the pub,
Was such a great fellow
Being told that he was wonderful
Whilst you, sitting at home,
Worried about every penny, fighting to survive
Until the stress of it laid you low, and you died.
Liz, you really and truly deserved a better life.

Back Again

You are here, you are back again,
Maybe you are just here to look around
Nothing much to see, then go ahead.

If you ever come back again
Do you think you will settle?
Become a person I can rely on?

If not, feel free to just look around,
Are you really back again?
Do I want or need you?
I think not, do not come back *Ever*,
You are not needed here.

Paedophile Man

Step aside, we can see inside morbid minds,
Internet grooming men that can't hide anymore.
You are ensnared in our net.
We are glancing inside your diseased mind,
We have dissected your labyrinth of deceit

Trespassed through into your web of images,
Nowadays no hiding place were you can retreat
Vile acts can't happen anymore, we can see
Inside your mind, not a healthy place to view.
Terrible images portrayed by hate filled minds,
Remember we can see inside your web.

No longer can we allow childish glee to be destroyed,
Apathy on our part is your defence, so step aside,
Remember through this medium of modern times
We are looking and finding you through our
Internet minds.

Assumption

He is, she is
What? How dare we assume?
How can we know anyone's thoughts, dreams,
Hopes, and aspirations? Yet we do! Who are we to assume?
Knowledge beyond our worth, how can we know
The heart and soul of everyone,
Or do we play that game?

You know the game of I bet you he is, she is, most certainly is,
Will do this, or that,
Make easy assumptions, all totally wrong.

Though they assuage our concept of being right by stroking inflated egos
Assuming the worse in others
Safer to assume, harder to be part of
Living decently, let's just assume.

Pontificate about people,
Nice, safe, mind numbing way to live
Just assume the worse about other people,
We can't be that bad.

Look at them bunch of ass...s.
I wonder if any assumptions are being made about us.
Of course not...
Safe assumption, I think not.

Garage Rules

No keys, no money, no exceptions.
No variances allowed.
No money, no keys, no car.
Simple rules, simply obey.
You ain't got the money
You don't get the car.
Rules unbreakable, you won't
Break me, I live by my rules.
No money, no keys, no exceptions,
Tell your story walking.
Man's got all the power, I've no car.
Have to accept without the dough, ray, me
I won't get far, have to think of a plan
Without exception. How about
We burn his yard he won't have power
But we won't have our car.
Need the dough, ray, me.
Gotta have my car, get the money,
Get my car, get acceptance,
Only way in life play by the man's rules.
No money, no keys, no car, no exceptions.

Simply You

You, you, quite simply you.
No one shall ever measure up to you.
Always a dream that I lived each day,
Every day you lived, loved, and enjoyed.
Happiness I attained loving you.
Every gesture, glance and touch made me joyful.
Each night, every moment I held you, gratitude.
Knowing and loving only you.

Simplicity

Your secret, so simple most of us
Find it unattainable, not you.
Living and loving in complete acceptance
Of being you. Most of us are other people.
Not you, life's secret obtained by accepting
Yourself as... *YOU.*

Drifting

Daylight over, there is nothing to fear.
All tomorrow's worries can be left for tomorrow.
Drift away and your dreams shall
Carry you beyond the stars.
No harm will befall you, no hurt will disturb you.

Drift gently into sleep
No one will know you
No one will judge you
No harm will befall you

After all, it's dreamtime.

The grace of sleep will comfort you,
That amazing place
Where trust and love prevail.

The night is warm, all around you is peaceful,
It's good to drift and let love protect you.
Sleep quietly, today is over,
No need to go back there.
Simply Dream, and go quietly
Beyond the starlight.

Evensong

Watched over by slow moving clouds
Day and evening gently embrace, as
The evening sunlight drapes itself
Languidly across pastoral hillsides.
Seeking out nocturnal visitors stirring restlessly
In their burrows, countryside and towns
Become one as the sun sets, letting mankind's mind calm.
Peace reigns if only momentarily, soft birdsong leads us
Into evening's calmness, and I sit and watch as
One peaceful day slips cheerfully into night's delightful end.
We can close the gate of today, and let tomorrow's worries be left
For tomorrow, let's sleep.

Spirit

Let me touch your spirit.
Life destroys so much of our inner selves
Though, if we touch each other's spirit
Perhaps then life that exists after death
Can revolve our around inner spirit
And we can and will ignore the slights
And hurts inflicted upon us by people not
Accepting that we never die, simply move
On to another level of God's wonderment.

Emma's Day Out

Sun's out, let's go for a drive.
Pass down by Lough side,
Heading out of town Whitehead looms large
Then the road drops down towards a
Sparkling sea where lighthouse island
Distantly hides behind Donaghadee.
Portmuck Pass's unseen Gobbins
Stonyand wild, what a nice day
To go for a drive.
Drive into port of Larne where ships nestling
Against the quay wait to ferry people
Out onto the placid sunny sea.
Drains bay starts the magnificent glens.
Wonderful scenery unfolds around
Each glorious bay, limestone cliffs
Stretch dangerous arms and funny auld signs
Predicting falls cause merriment,
What a lovely day to go for a drive.
Ballygally castle, picnic tables and swings
Whilst out to sea strange rocks... are they
Ships or submarines, isn't it great going for a drive?
Ballygally left behind, its castle gone,
On to Glenarm with it's small harbour,
Cruise over the bridge, nine glens there to wander,
Drive into Carnlough, its deep water harbour
Packed with boats, on to Waterfoot pass Carndhu
Where Old Man rock for eons has stood, battered by storms,
Kissed gently today by sunny seas. Drive up to Glenariff,
Stroll up to Laragh Falls and Corrib, then into Cushendall,
Have a stop for tea, isn't it nice to go for a drive?

this poem was written about the Glens of Antrim, 21 years ago. My youngest girl, Emma, asked me to not take her to school and just go for a drive. Being silly, I took her to school, and all the way to work regretted my decision. To make it up to her I wrote this poem at work, for her.

Old Times / New Times

The Century passed as if it was a bird on the wing.
Momentary uplifts in the eons of time.
Recorded incidents of great import.
Now only remembered in history lessons.
Wars, killing fields forgotten, and the century
Swept like the bird on the wing never pausing
To reflect on the lonely hours spent gazing at the past.
Yesterday's headline, tomorrow's sorrow, no change,
Only the end of one millennium and the same old
Routine starts over, and we accept it as mankind's due.
Though, were is the love in life that we promised
Ourselves? Is it lost in the mists of time?
That one moment when we climbed hills and
Stood together holding hands, thinking we had all the world
At our feet. The century has glided past.
Now we no longer soar as the bird on the wing.
Simply accept that time has passed, and we have
Moved on as the century closed its door on old lovers.

Broken Leaves

Walking through the deserted landscape
Of my mind, I find myself wishing
For one more day. One moment to
Clarify the time that once meant so
Much to me - being with you.

Simple moments when we strolled and hugged, as
Sunlight eased its way through the branches of trees
Casting shadows on broken leaves, and we
Arm in arm spoke quietly to one another.
Now realizing that I never once
Said I love you, always hiding from?
Imagined slights and hurts, this is where I end.

Wishing for one more day to spend with you.
To tell you I love you, now knowing that had I held you
And asked do you love me we might be together.
Instead, here I end kicking my way through
Broken Leaves, the sunlight
Casting shadows as it tears my heart apart.

But I'm lost in those shadows as I think of you,
And all I had to do was say - I love you.
I think often of those three words -
I love you. Simple to utter, complexities in
Their simplicity. Wondering had I asked you,
Would I be kicking my way through these
Wind-blown leaves wishing
For that elusive, one more day with you?

Broken Strings

Had a quiet night, so peaceful
In my room, not a sound disturbed
Me. Difficult to realise,
Driving down the street in the morning
That a family string had been broken,
Father bloody battered and broken,
Dead upon arrival. All over a fag. Such
A tragedy over 30 pence of tobacco.
A family man walking homewards after a night out.
And me so peaceful in my room, whilst
Down the street murder and grief for a family.
So easily the strings are broken, yet what
Has happened in our society if a life is not
Even worth more than a cigarette?
This is not a fanciful thought, it happened on 22-04-2010 as it does
Every night whilst most of us are lying quietly
In our peaceful rooms, and broken strings of
Finely woven family threads are pulled asunder
And shall resonate forever in all our lives.
How can we, the society that has created these useless hoods
Stand quiet as they strut about?

Players

With great regret we watch
As players leave the stage of life.
Some we knew, others we loved,
Most we had never met, they simply
Strolled off stage their performance.
We miss each and every one enacted out.
Great drama enriching our lives
With their unequalled valour, showing us
The actor's great dedication to the art of living.
Sadly, those we loved and the ones we hardly knew
They walked away from centre stage.
Small or large parts, whichever they played left an
Everlasting impression in our lives
Leaving us with a parting gift - peace and
Common good to all in their final scene
And we, the actors, play our part laying a wreath,
Bowing our heads as they walk off stage.

Hoods Morality

looking out of hooded eyes
they have, he has, she has.
we're taking whatever we want
we'll take, that's our work.
destroying their lives.

we want, they, him, her.
you have what we want.
we will kill
wreck, ruin to take
that which is yours.

don't think we won't.
we're hoods, morons.
though being without morals
we kill, wreck, and ruin lives to
take the joy.

you've worked, saved,
went without. we take what we want.
who's to stop us, underage you see?
police? *Joke, Men.*
no one stops us.

we take whatever we want.
You! Them, Him, Her,
only there to serve us.
we, the vice ridden men
take all and everything
we want!

Face Value

How many times have you opened
Your heart and home to someone
Only to have it rejected in an underhanded way?
This aspect of taking and trusting at face value
Is dangerous to our well being, it wanders around in
Your mind wrecking all trust in humanity.

All right, we can get it wrong but when
We are told it's ok, nothing wrong with us,
And we accept people into our homes
On trust, sometimes, if not at all times
We have to look at our motives for helping.
Are they as altruistic as we think? Perhaps

It helps us to seem better than our neighbour.
We do all we can, then realise they have wronged us
Who then is right - you, him, her? We took all
At face value only to find they are nothing people.
I guess, at the end of days, it was better to do something.

Today's Wigan Pier / A Parody of Orwell

Thugs abound today, kicking their
Filth around. They complain, oh, how
They love to complain - we have nothing,
Whine and whine as they slug down the
Cheap supermarket wine.

Kicking their filth into palatial rat holes
Given to them by tax payers' money,
Unlike the hungry thirties.
Then, poverty meant drawing an allowance from the P.A.C.
Measuring up to the mean's test, it always caused
Despair no work. No dole, only the cold, cold test.
If you didn't kow-tow to the state's "gratitude"

Thrown out of your home. Now the great-grandsons
Are not a people, only scum crawling through
People's lives pleading for their dole and D.L.A.
Screeching we have nothing, with beseeching hands
Outstretched to steal your last penny they cry
We have only three bedrooms one bathroom,

One dole drop to collect our pregnant girl's money
Before she gets it and wastes it on that bloody child,
Cheek of her buying food to feed a hungry child,
We need our fix - alcohol, drugs out of our heads,
This is the way to live in splendour thinking
She will miss me when I'm gone.

Their forefathers had no work, poverty "justified"
By the state, do you really expect the youth of today
To work, are you nuts? The state
Is for the layabout, we are on the take,
Small minded men.
We hate *All The People*.

Halloween

Halloween,
Please put a penny in the old man's hat
It's Halloween, all souls night,
Bright moon-light sky allowing all souls to
Watch as we celebrate witches sweeping along streets
On plastic brooms knocking on our hearts
Asking for a halfpenny, even an apple will do,
Night's sky exploding into glorious light
Highlighting transparent souls weeping into our dreams
Old time memories precluding any harm as each witch
Transmogrifies into our children,
All souls watching, and smiling,
Dreaming their dreams of yesterday.
Please, put a penny in the old man's hat,
If you haven't got a penny a halfpenny
Will do, if you haven't a halfpenny God bless you,
It's Halloween, all souls night

Because of You

Because of you I drifted
Where sunlight always shone,
Watching its soft, rose hue garland.
You made me believe
That because of loving you
Living is worthwhile.

Mr. and Mrs. Blah

Went to a meeting, listened to the speakers,
Very interesting observations
Every point made was
Blah, blah, blah
Good points lot of wisdom.

I decided to seek clarification
They elucidated, blah, blah, blah
I acknowledged each point and
Their right to speak, even if is a bit obscure.

Though, for the life of me, I
Cannot understand their logic
In blah, blah, blah.
On the way out had my hand shook
By Mr. and Mrs. Blah thanking me effusively
In their most mannerly blah for listening.

I said, with great aplomb I might add,
Thank you, and blah, blah, blah
As you can ascertain I tire of all the
Bollocks one hears at meetings, even if
It is only a load of blah, blah, blah.

Moonlight

You are beautiful tonight,
Your ambient light
Gracing the night's sky.
Such a wondrous sight
Glowing cheerfully against
Night's ebony, silent sky
Embracing all
Who happily accept
Living in God's given grace, and just
For a moment I'm reminded
That's life's reflections,
In peaceful minds
Shall cause us no harm.

Let us live happily
And know that you
Are God's given beauty
And all we have to do
Is take our eyes
From the ground
And embrace the moonlight.

Longing

I glanced away, and
You were gone.
As if an early mist had
Been burned away
By morning sunlight,

Though, knowing within my soul
You had roiled away
Into God's all forgiving embrace.
I wandered and watched
Until night drew in
Then I chanced upon the stars.

You, my darling girl
Had reappeared, laughing
Mischievously among
The cumulus,
I glance away
And look back,

You are still there.
On diamond nights
You can always be seen
Dancing, laughing, and
Playing among the starlight.

Letter in a Box

Words on paper, lined and highlighted
Found years later, let thoughts of
Fond memories flood into my mind
Happy times spent in years past
Remembered through letters in a box.

Thoughts sent from friends, some forgotten
Others no longer with me, long since departed
These letters found in a box remind me
That friends are with us always. Never
Really letting go of yesterdays, we simply
Let time become a comrade in arms

The old friends could have been, and 'if only'
No longer means anything. Years have passed, the
Old friends have gone, only reality left is
Sifting long ago memories found in an
Old letters box.

Dancing in the Shadow of the Wind

Whilst the wind has stilled, shall we
Dance joyfully in the shadows of
Today because tomorrow our
Old friends fade gently away?

So let's dance whilst we can in the shadows
Of the wind, and listen to the chimes of yesterday
As we sway gracefully in harmony
With the shadows of our dreams

Seeking only those
Memories that still the gales in our heart, remembering
All the old friends that once danced with us whilst
The winds of yesterday blew carelessly through our lives

Letting us grasp our tomorrows as if all
The old and new times would remain, and the winds of
Today give solace to the shadows in our lives.

Now we, few who remain, smile in remembrance of all
The old friends who swept through our lives, and left deep
Shadows in the stillness of the wind.

Mumbia

Screams suddenly erupt out of
Fright filled minds as bodies curl
In anticipation of dying, bullets thud
All around, and death's grim scythe
Sweeps through the flotsam of human debris.

No quarter given none can be sought
The dead cannot stop the reaper's task
Once again a heart wrenching sigh echoes
Around the world as Hezbollah state the
Blood is on Hindu hands.

Are they right, are they wrong?
Ask the hundred locked in death
Behind the reaper's mask, the blood of the
Dead shall soon be cleansed though how
Long before the innocent can heal.

Belfast, City of Madness

Terrified screams cast a
Black shroud cover over city streets.
Day and night Belfast screams,
Building slowly then ending in
Death and punishment beatings.
Belfast, City of Madness,
Hammers pound in its people's minds
Siren calls to commit murder.
Staccato murmurs creep along its
City streets throwing up gutter thoughts.
Come, dance in our mayhem, enjoy
Belfast, City of Madness.

Fateful Night

You stopped by late that night, and
I didn't ask as I should have,
Are you alright, wished that I had asked you
To stay, who knows, we may have chatted
The night away.

Why didn't I ask on that fateful night
Are you alright, must have been
Too caught up in myself, now as I stare
Down the years and remember your
Haunted look, I always ask myself why,
Why didn't I ask you to stay and hold you tight?

Say stay, you'll be alright. Instead I let you
Walk away. I recall you paused, pity that I
Never called out. My heart is weary as
Thinking back all it needed was that one query,
Who knows, it might have saved your life,
Are you alright?

Back When

Let's fly back to before we needed or wanted
To grow up, back to the days
I strolled Black Mountain,
Ran free in the bog meadows.
They put me in school and I wasted my time

Should have left me to run free.
All of my life shaped by moments
Spent alone contented and at peace,
Roaming Divis or playing in the bog meadows.

Now, flying down along this freedom road, I cannot forget
People and places, mostly gone now or lost in the mists of time,
Holiday months spent joyfully on farms,
Time spent in school
I couldn't understand - multiply, subtract or divide
I simply didn't want to know,

I would rather run free
Amongst the beauty of the hillside, and meadow.
Saving grace was boy scouts,
Clonard con fraternity
And then McCances glen
With its' dark flowing waters,

Wonderment days walking
Homewards, elated, soaked to the skin,
Simple times, should have left me to run free

Never wanted to grow up.
But, of course I did.
Accepted responsibility.
Didn't do too bad
All in, just did the best I could

And now, nearing the end of my time, how I wish
That once more I was running free
Over Divis and bog meadows.

Angels Caring

Not only angels can fly so high
Let us look beyond ourselves and see
How high we can soar, forgetting self
Thinking of others reaching our hand
Help a stranger along

We all can be angels if we care for each other
Forgetting self, raise up your head
You can soar on high, without fear
Only caring and sharing with the world

Remember, we all can be angels. Reach out
And help that stranger along
You will soar on high with angels' wings
Nothing can stop you

If you let go and fly
No blame game, only loving and caring
Wouldn't that be a change?
Let's fly, let's all soar high on angels' wings.

I Wonder

It was so good to see you.
Seems a long time since you called by
Though, lying here where I should not be,
In a hospital bed, I wonder do you love me?

I truly love you, yet, I often lie crying and
Wondering - do you love me? That nagging
Question is destroying me quicker than my illness,
Hold me, and tell me that you truly love me

As I slip into this everlasting sleep, at peace,
Knowing you love me and I, well, I have always loved you.
Though this mantra of do you love me, do you love me
Gives me no freedom
To embrace these last, dark days.

Footsteps murmuring in tranquil
Chapels form echoes of childhood
Memories.
In my mind those forgotten
Moments brought forward in the sudden
Rush of incense letting thoughts of old
Friends, resonate in joyful glory.

Those youthful echoes of games played
In innocent moments sweep me down
Along weary corridors, lined
And aged in my mind
Though sitting happily, reflecting, enjoying
Moments of the past.

Realising it's never forgotten,
Only momentarily set aside
To be resurrected as I
Listen to footsteps echoing among the transept
In the tranquillity of chapel.

American Diplomacy

We shall sort out this world problem
Diplomatically,
If you won't listen to our threats
We will sort you out of course,
Diplomatically.

Nuclear missiles carry lots of weight,
We shall drop in on you.
Diplomatically.

Sort your problem out once and for all
Though, upon reflection, we created your problem
Diplomatically

Can't ever admit that, we are never wrong
Wouldn't do to show weakness
Diplomatically,
We will just sort of destroy you.

Start over with another one
With lots of oil, we shall sort them out
Diplomatically.

Waltz

Life is a waltz and we,
The dancers, circling memories
In the ballroom of shadows.
Imagine subtle shades of light
Reflect people and places
Though, as we circle,
Always shadows leave memories of love
In this, our waltz with life.
Dancers never stop.
Music carries dreams and lost loves.
So the waltz shall always continue
Whilst dreams and memories cast
Shadows into our waltz with life.

Indifferent

Turn it on, hear the news.
See what death toll we have today.
Watch the buildings raze to an indifferent ground.
Watch the bodies as they tumble down,
Ignore beseeching eyes set in small,
Fearful faces.
Just turn it on, watch the death toll mount -
After all it's over there, not here.
Let's simply ignore those pleading, screaming eyes
Ignore hunger, hurt, and pain,
A cup of tea you say, o aye, that'll do,
Let's watch the news, turn it on.

Weary

You closed your eyes, said you
Felt weary, needed a moment's peace.
Slipped off to sleep never realising
Your God you would meet.
I'm sure he smiled, clasped your hand
And whispered we have been waiting
For you to slip away into that nice cosy sleep,
Into God's world you step serene, pain and despair gone,
Eyes dancing in your head once again as
You glide amongst long gone friends. They,
Like you, felt weary though had a moment's sleep
And now, like you, they have found eternal peace.

Serious

What reason do we have for
Being so very serious?
Is it because we believe it's only
Way to live? Should know
Better. Can't
Love when we are so serious or
Laugh and play.
Nope, we can
Only be serious.
Stand and watch a sun-shower
Thinking - wish it would stop,
Can't see the beauty
In the fresh
Smell from the tarmac, nope,
We can only be serious
And see the gloom in today.
Worst of it is we will only
See gloom tomorrow.
Relax, it's only living,
Are we really that important?
Don't believe so, in fact - I know so.

Today is Different

We kill more effectively,
Even God manages to die today.
De-foliate, deforestation words describing
Inhuman acts against nature, God's work
We kill, and he dies. One wonders
When his avenging hand will fall.
Then we, fools, shall truly know the sound of
One hand clapping whoever this god fellow is.
Governments hold him in high esteem, yet
Kill his wonders quietly and efficiently,
They evoke his name, in God we trust, to destroy our
Homeland, they call upon us "the people"
To justify killing in his name, one wrong,
One slight and going
To war can make it right, they demonstrate their might.
Their God is no different from our yesterdays, when
They killed effectively with silent crossbow
And declared the world's end, and even earlier
They put him on a cross, and killed him and
Today we still mutter "in God we trust".

Unseen

In dead men's clothes we steal away unseen,
Through trenches were ramparts burst apart
With shellfire, knowing only death awaits us
In this hellish place we call no man's land.

Each day and night bone cold and weary as only
Dead men's minds could be,
We bless each moment as another shell shrieks past.
Selfishly thanking our God that we have survived another day.
And we, the unseen,
Steal away watching the morning sun.
It blushes the poppies crimson

Same shade as our fallen comrades' blood.
We stare with pitied eyes as the stretcher maimed
Are carried away to spend their days in endless pain.
And now, the new dead of today are once more urged
Forwards, and lament as we cast ourselves
In futile gesture upon our unseen enemies' guns.

Wasted Lives

Rows of glasses, having plenty of good time
Or so we imagined, ignoring the publican
Shouting time, doesn't he know?
This is our moment in time, rows of
Glasses and broken lives.

Always we thought there would be lots of time.
Speaking aimlessly, drinking shamelessly,
Now looking inwards at cosy reflections
All that's left are rows of glasses and
Fair weather friends, family forgotten.

Only drinking not thinking of the real time ahead
Pub door slams, on your own, this is reality,
Family gone, cold room, colder hearth
No cosy reflections of loved ones, their
Faces swimming in memory. Have another drink,
You're on your own, cannot face real time.

Big City Time

One minute equals one hour in
Big city time, three hours become
Three days, no time to think,
You don't own your mind, it's on
Loan to the City, we need more hours.

Days are too short, can't stop,
We are on the clock,
What are you doing thinking,
Don't, you're wasting time,
In the city it's hurry up, hurry up, run, run.

You're on the treadmill,
Can't complain your choice
Just do, keep on surviving,
Buddy can you spare a dime,
Take no notice, it's only a bum.

No pity given, takes time to care,
This is reality,
Big City hustle,
Time's awaiting,
And we're living it all

Flight

Are we to be refugees?
To struggle and fight
Then rush headlong into flight
Our meagre belongings strewn
Throughout this violent land
No homes or hearths welcome us
No songs are sung to honour us
We are the victims in this city
Of sorrows, only the warriors have their songs
Ah, but to think when they are gone
We the refugees remain, always doing
Battle with our constant enemy - hunger.

Life, Maybe, Perhaps

I live a life of delicate lies
Built on gossamer webs,
Tissue built then destroyed
Lives on in memories of
Schemes lost.

Well, God called you, I can be
Selfish and ask why you, though,
Then I condemn someone else.

I question the God why he decided on you.
It seems only the meek
And the good die young,
I don't for one minute
Subscribe to the meek shall inherit the world look
Around all the cretins
Who are running the world.

So, once again, I ask why you.
If I get into acceptance
Then I guess the world
Is an uncertain and poorly thought out
Place. God gave us choice

And a beautiful planet,
It's just we adore the gladiators.
Let's leave the arena and
Look after the meek. Problem is
Elitism always wins.

Don't Think

Strange how things have changed.
Not just gone tomorrow,
forgotten today... We absorb, absolve,
then abandon thoughts, ideas litter
our lives, clutter. Sweep them aside,
They were thoughts of a moment ago.
Did you write them down? Couldn't,
Old ways, Computer is down.
Just as well might have gone through
Hell. Thinking, bad for you, me, us...
Everyone. Can't hang on to old ways,
even Orwell got it wrong, he thought
old ways '84, should try today.
Even big brother's on TV... *Must Be True*.
New ways cannot be swept aside,
media free thinkers, they are not cancerous,
we have been given our Utopian society.
Mustn't let free thinkers usurp our
sheepish ways.

Yesterday's Man

driving through a yesterday land
I chanced upon a yesterday man
gazing forlorn at his yesterday home
its cold boarded up look belied
the warmth in its yesterday hearth.
love and affection, stories and songs
lost to future despair.
yesterday's country folk gone
no more easy talk or
slow moving carts, only
fast cars never slowing to
reflect on a yesterday man
gazing at his yesterday home.

Immigrants' Souls

We're on full alert waiting, circling
in the dark as all predators do.
We seek survival, arrival,
our families are hungry, hurting.
We must succeed, they are life,
one of us, and we are one.
In the darkness we circle our prey,
gargantuan monsters of myth,
belching steam and smoke from
their mouths and underbellies.
An opening, any sort, loose flap,
door not sealed. We must succeed
Our prey England, Ireland.
These beasts we circle in the night,
our lifeline to another life.
We work to assuage our families' hurt.
We must succeed, no if only.
When our chance comes, we attack
sliding into the monsters underbelly,
slipping down its throat.
We must bring down this channel
of water, we have to win.
We live our life as immigrant souls
No helping hand, only servitude awaits.
From all over Europe we set out.

Striving to find our mentors, union men, gone!
Only employers circling, we are prey,
road kill, carrion. Cast aside to rot
in government indifference.
Scorned, denied any rights, fellow workers
turn away muttering in their pubs and clubs
these immigrants work for nothing.
Not the fault of immigrant hearts.

We must succeed to feed our families.
Unions gone, no solidarity, Thatcherism
whispers, murmurs through our souls,
working man's rights destroyed.
No union rights, powerless, you are prey.
Seek the just man whose words of wisdom
shall set us free, defeating our masters.
Letting us snap these chains of servitude,
we must become part of an immigrant heart.

The Burning Man

I sit, thinking I'm at the end.
Not the end of time itself,
Plainly the end of ever writing.
I keep thinking of the line, the burning man perhaps,
That's simply me wanting to write again.
So here I am, trying to burn once more.

If I stop caring about my failings and think less
Of what others say about me perhaps I will
Once again get down on paper how I feel
And stop burning up inside,
Feeling I'm to old to write,
It's all in the past.
Instead let's shout I'm still about,
After all they are only
Thoughts of my own, not what others imagine.

When the idea springs to mind,
That intrinsic moment
Then dismiss it, that's when
I know I'm burning up inside.
Here I sit, trying to write myself back into
Doing, and stop my musing
Upon the end of time.

I look back, and realise
It's only words on paper,
Some may enjoy, and some may
Despair at my folly,
There are those who
Do not understand the concept of a
Moment in time

When we need time to ourselves, and
Here I am, the burning man,
Trying to take time and write again.
I shall write, good or bad, how I don't care.

Hi

How are you feeling?
Is it just another night, are you
Drifting with old, new friends?
If I listen hard enough I might
Hear you all laughing, shouting.

If I don't see you again I'll know
You are always young, cruising along on
A never-ending night, I know your lot
Flowing effortlessly through time
Have got it right, but I
Miss you, what can I say, you had to go
It can be long nights here listening to you
Sitting by my shoulder "unseen".
Guess I shouldn't go there, but I miss you when my
Heart is misbehaving, and loving you, having
To stay here, hoping once again we'll meet
Up, then go cruising with old, new friends on
Another glorious never-ending night.

Immoralist

Dye the bloody hand of Ulster in Fenian blood,
Who is this mad cleric that he exhorts loyalist mobs
To commit such heinous acts, why
Does this Mr. Paisley think he has a right to condemn
Righteous people to death in the name of Ulster?
Is he prepared to die for his inglorious cause?
This D.U.P. lout screams no so loudly that's others of his
Ilk are prepared to dye their hands his political
Slogan K.A.T. couched in NO. Today we shall march
Trampling on so called Fenians' rights, the right to parity
Of esteem not in D.U.P. parlance,
Mr. Paisley Declares You Shall Die Tonight.
Dye, dye the bloody hand of these six counties bright red
Protestant might, what right this parody of clerical imagery
To lay claim to one of proud Rosaleen's provinces?
Paisley's joy to watch as Ulster's rightful people die, he
Lines his coffers bright whilst the mob he exhorts
Live in their hovels proud of the slogan K.A.T.
He screams loudly kill, kill them tonight, no surrender,
He cares nothing for his victim's plight,
Darkly clad, white collar shining bright he screams loudly K.A.T.
We shall see you tonight.

The initials K.A.T. stand for Kill All Taigs, the term taigs being a slang term used by Protestants to describe Catholics. And Mr. Paisley is the mad cleric directly responsible for all the catholic deaths in Northern Ireland over these last 40 years of warfare. Fenians is another slang term for Catholics.

D.U.P. Democratic Unionist Party, founded by Ian Paisley.

Nuclear

In a field of flowers, when soft winds
Bend delicate stalks of gossamer green
Insects of myriad variety touch lightly
Upon each flower, take what's needed.
Then flit gently away.
Destruction left to man, never content
He rapes the flowers with hot winds
Of nuclear power, life decimated.

Love Never Ages

Love never ages, only people age.
Love is a lifetime of sharing and caring,
Love itself can never grow old, only the
Passage of time makes people grow old.
As we, the people, grow old love becomes
Affection, the passion of youth may have gone
But love, it never ages. Only people age.

Dark Night

Lonely the road travelled alone
Imagination on overdrive creating
A plethora of characters,
Marley's ghost rattling chains, siren calls
Pulling you forwards, phantoms on your mind
Vividly seen with each new step,
Darkness hiding trolls on the long dark road
Of the soul, darkling bush with eerie soughing musical
Chords scraping across long discarded statuesque forms
In deserted bowers brings myths alive in ebony
Blue black sky and I cast glowering glances
Upon each new pothole stumbling into hellish
Nightmarish arms, falling endlessly, grim reaper's
Scythe sweeping your face, during daylight only that benign
Bloodless bush, now Bosh demon death's cape on,
Fearsome lonely road, soft light spied ahead such relief
As you embrace familiar voices wondering why
You set out on darkling road, after all
You only wanted a pint of beer

Awhile

You are only gone awhile, Liz,
Still I listen for your laughter
Search for your ready smile
It seems a longish time, though
I know you have only left
Even if you stay away awhile
The beauty of you is in my mind, it shall stay forever.

Days we walked and talked
You would go away awhile
Was not a long time
Now you have passed away
I will miss you for longer than awhile
Hush, you are only to be gone awhile, wee Liz.

Hidden Valley / Alice Springs, 2006

What price must we pay for freedom
In our land, what price must we pay in
Our aboriginal children's loss of life,
What price will we have paid when our
Tears have dried, what price will future
Generations pay for the vanishing shadows
Of justice, what price have we paid for the
Genocide of our people?
What price are we asked to pay to be a part of
Australia?
Ask yourself this - is this price enough: brutal deaths,
Rape, murder, hunger, poverty?
What price must we pay for our heritage?

This Is Australia, Our Land.

Once in Belfast

this was the Belfast of the 1960 era, if you were around, then the innocent times were ending

Days of belted raincoats, hair bobbed in style.
Astor, Romanoes, Jig and Ceili, all
Dance halls, dreams.
Hands held in picture halls.
Lingering nights ending at shimmering dawns.

Working days swiftly passing, slow Saturdays strolling.
Lambrettas, Morris cars, youth hostels.
Walking miles. Lasting moments.
Days of belted raincoats.
Stroll along Royal Avenue, Farset hidden.
Follow its path to Woolworth's doors.
Albert Clock, slightly worse for wear.

Drift down Pottingers' entry.
Morning Star, shining bright.
Ann Street thronged with goose bumped
Thighs glorified in mini skirts.
Mooney's Pub watching over corn market,
Draught horses and Guinness.

Bible thumpers, selling Jesus no one listening.
Days of innocence.
Years may have passed, tracksuits and attitude all around.
Was it only yesterday we wandered down town?
Now planners and people's wrath wreaked
On memories hang up that belted raincoat.
We'll just sit down. Long before the innocent can heal.

Relentless

And the children died.
They, our children fought and they died.
Then our children's children
Picked up the gun, and the struggle continued
Whether it is in Belfast, Palestine,
Ecuador, and Afghanistan - our children
Are relentless, and they died
Whilst throughout the world moneyed powered
Baron enjoined to force their farce of alien
Government upon a righteous people.
The bloodied years passed, our children's
Bodies amassed, on hunger strike they died
Whilst we listened to the lies of politicians
Demanding that "we the people" accept
Their burning *Bush*.
And the children died, now we have grown old
And become grandparents, nothing changes
Our children are still dying...

Written in memory of the men and women on hunger strike in H-Blocks and Armagh, N.Ireland/6 counties

Smile

Let me smile each day, and remind me always
That I carry your smile in my heart,
The smile on my lips and the merriment
In my eyes is caused by having known and
Loved you, this smile today is that once again
I'm reminded of our yesterdays, and my tomorrows are
But more memories to store warmly beside your smile that
I shall always carry in my heart, passionately aware
That it was God's blessing to have given me the gift of
Meeting and loving you, so just for today let me
Smile, even though you have passed away,
wee Liz.

To Have Lived the Dream

If you find love in your lifetime
Then all eternity is yours, the promise
Of eternal life is realised, how you lived your
Life shall be forever remembered and all that's
Required is to have loved and have shown love.
Love is not just a word, it is a thought, action, deed,
And above all else passion. Try not to let destroyed
Spirits create hate, lust, greed and ignorance, none of
These emotions inspire love, to say I love you
And mean it is the greatest appreciation you can offer in life.
I have lived, I have loved, and in having achieved
That dream I received all the joy of living and grieving.
When you love there is always that heart stopping moment
When death embraces the one you love, that is when you
Have to accept they shall live for ever, why? because love never dies.
The magical spirit of your love remains imbedded in
Their soul, and when you move on and meet once again
Then always love left behind means you have never truly died.
You have lived, and left the meaning of life behind (*Love*).

Moments in Time

Children play innocent games
Running, laughing, shouts of glee.
Skipping ropes slap the ground.
No horror played out, just shouts of glee,
Innocents in time.
Fleeting moments held
And cherished, suddenly
Silence reigns,
No voices raised
Just a glowing screen
Where voices once ran
In joyful fun.
Innocence, like a butterfly, has a
Short span of life.

A Terrible Beauty

Love is pain
A terrible beauty we cannot live without

Love is life itself
Adventurous and daring in its passion

The true essences of love and living
Is in caring thoughts of others

That singular moment when you reach
Out your hand and say - I love you

Bestows wealth and wisdom
Beyond our understanding

Love is a life fulfilled,
A terrible beauty, love.

Imprint My Love

If my soul had fingers
I would ask it to depart and
Touch you lightly upon your
True, true heart, and with that touch
I would imprint my love.
And you shall know that one day I will arrive,
Then like souls in flight we shall depart.
And for all eternity our fingers shall
Remain entwined, forever around our loving hearts.

Shake Hands with My Heart

Shake hands with my heart,
Sit down and let's talk awhile.
You don't seem to come around
As often, was it something I said
That drove us apart?

I can't recall having offended you
Though, that's often my lot, not thinking
Before destroying another's heart.
Sit awhile and talk, sure it can't
Hurt to smile and say hello.

I'm thinking wouldn't it be nice
If once again you shook hands
With my heart?
Not often I get the chance to
Say how much I missed you.
Please don't go, sit awhile,

Whilst I try to explain how much
I regret the time we have spent apart.
Such fond memories of being with you,
Those quiet times that went drifting by
Sharing our love, and dreaming dreams together.
Please, sit and once again shake hands
With my heart.

No Man's Land

Shells exploding, my world imploding.
Confined in living graves we survive.
Bodies underfoot elevating me, the zombie
To lethargic heights, and I strain to hear that final blast.
One long shrieking whistle hurtling forwards to me
Into that no man's land. It's a land of turmoil, death,
Glory, where mythical wonders expounded at clean,
Initial-scarred desks denied the ugliness of

War's grim reality, your boyhood intestines
Sliding into gore filled ground. So much for conquest.
Story books and songs of valour, another dead friend,
Only survival as death slips by, his sting whispering
Inanely past your ear, busy bugles' calls trawling us forwards
Whilst we are sprawled in mud wishing I was once again foetus
Only formed in womb not to be misshapen in death that
Even a casket disdains your deformed body.

Only the unmarked grave of the Unknown Soldier where
Future generations shall salute you
In clean surroundings, little caring that you are
Still in that final no man's land, looping your innards
Into heaven's gate, not only the dead can carry a tale.
Those left alive can tell that war is truly hell.
If we stand in no man's land, ghostly spectres are
Carried along on lone bugler's wail
Lost finally in an imploding grave.

Truth

What is truth, is it your truth,
My truth, to whom does truth belong?
Is it politicians, governments, clergy,
Or does truth belong to the "people"?
Perhaps truth belongs to those who
Create the falsehood of their truth.
When we, the "people", search for truth we
Become lost in the falsehoods of centuries.
Machiavelli was the master of deception
Though was cruelty and bad faith his truth?
And were do the "people" search for life's truths?
In our hearts, and our souls, and in what we are told
Or read as we might accept, and I emphasize *might*,
Should become the chief law of all the "people".

No Epitaph

No one shall write an epitaph of me.
I shall not let anyone close enough to know me.
I wander alone amongst strangers in
The deep canyons of city streets, ignoring
The ebb and flow of humanity.
Strolling causally, avoiding contact,
A stranger in a strange town.
No epitaph could nor would be written.
Simply because the city and I are
An unsuitable alliance.

Provisional Honour

The blood of heroes flowed through this land
And we cannot forget that we nurtured
All the warriors. Now we, the people, ask
Who are these carpetbagger warriors
That venerate the English government?

On every street in Belfast heroes' blood was shed,
What answers can they now offer our warrior dead?
The blood of our warrior dead has been washed
Into sewers by self-seeking politicians,
Those same ones who often sought succour and
Professed to be part of the struggle.

Minders and protectors of the people:
What runs through the veins of these limousine
Riding warriors, not our heroes' blood, most likely
Their good lunch and whatever perfidy they are waging
Against we, the people who once let them carry the
Blood of our children away on regurgitated lies.

What price is put on freedom when the so called warriors
Become part of the establishment, tottering along on
Rotten foundations, what price honour as we watch
The blood of our warriors being wasted for a paltry
Thirty shillings.

Love Redeems All

The river of love runs deep.
The river of love runs swift.
The river of love runs forever.

Love should be patience.
Love should endless.
Love should be passionate.
Love should be profound.

There are times when time itself
Makes love a travesty.
Love can become destructive.
Love can be unhinged.
Love can be obscene.

Though love of the heart,
Love of the mind,
Love of the soul,
Love of accepting each other
Can't ever be imperfect.

Without love the humanness of people
Would forever cease to exist.
Love is pure
Love is faithful
Love is sincere
Love is gallant.

The river of love sweeps all other
Emotions aside, true love redeems all,
Love never ages.
Only people, age.

One More Night

Let's dance together one more night.
Even though you're now someone else's lover
Fold me in your arms.
Hold me tightly and let's dance, even if
It's only for tonight.

We can feel as if we are in paradise
And this shall last for all eternity
Though I know it's only for tonight.
This old palace of dreams I thought would
Never crumble lies in ruins, an empty shell,
Hold me and dance.

As you slip quietly away, I shall sway
Dreamily, believing you are still mine.
You have closed the door to my heart and I
Dancing to the music of another time, believing
These palace walls hide my dreams.
Cannot accept there will never be one more night.

www.ingramcontent.com/pod-product-compliance
Lightning Source LLC
Chambersburg PA
CBHW062203080426
42734CB00010B/1771